ASSASSIN'S CREED™

1 | DESMOND

STORY : CORBEYRAN
ART : DJILLALI DEFALI
COLOR : RAPHAEL HEDON,
MADEMOISELLE K & KNESS

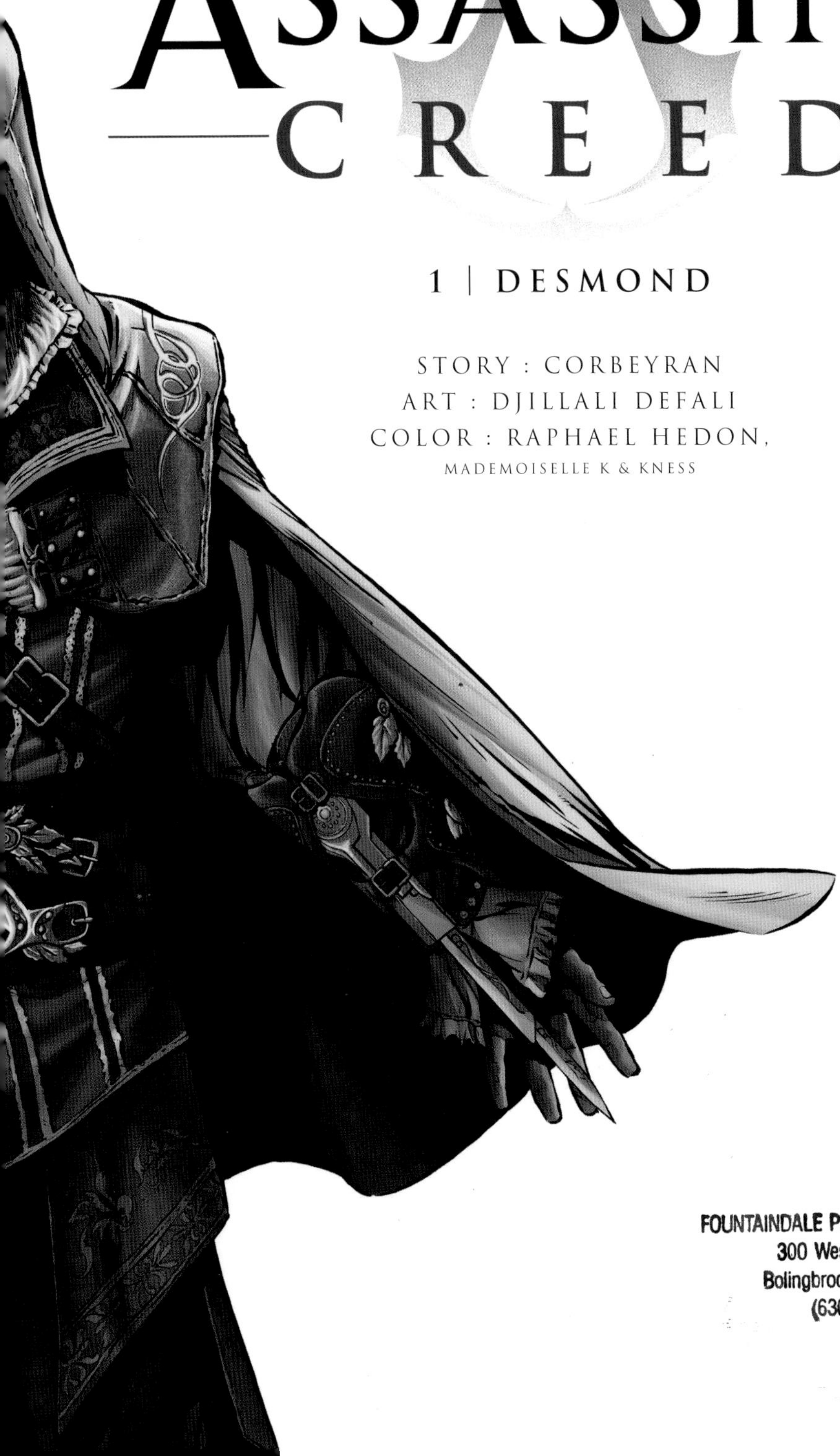

ASSASSIN'S CREED: DESMOND

ISBN: 9781781163405

Published by Titan Books
A division of Titan Publishing Group Ltd.
144 Southwark St.
London
SE1 0UP

Les Deux Royaumes | Ubisoft France | 173-179 rue du Chevaleret | 75 646 Paris Cedex 13

First Titan edition: October 2012
English-language translation: Mark McKenzie-Ray

A CIP catalogue record for this title is available from the British Library

10 9 8 7 6 5 4 3

Printed in the United States of America

What did you think of this book? We love to hear from our readers. Please email us at: readerfeedback@titanemail.com, or write to us at the above address. To receive advance information, news, competitions, and exclusive offers online, please sign up for the Titan newsletter on our website: www.titanbooks.com

ACKNOWLEDGMENTS

Thank you to Djillali Defali for setting me on this fascinating adventure. To Alexis Nolent for being my guide and accompanying me through this new territory. Thanks also to François Tallec, Olivier Henriot and Geoffroy Sardi, as well as the teams at Ubisoft Paris and Montreal, for opening their doors and welcoming me into this universe.

CORBEYRAN

Thank you to Matz for the phone call, even if you regretted it afterwards, I didn't let you down, buddy! Thanks to the whole team at Ubisoft Montreal for their time and patience. Benjamin Dennel – thank you, my friend, for the motivation and encouragement. And a huge thanks to François Tallec, for supporting me during the creation of the album – I know it wasn't easy!

DEFALI

Thank you to Yves Guillemot, Alain Corre, Serge Hascoet, Jade Raymond, Patrice Desilets, Corey May, Sébastien Puel, Mohamed Gambouz, Olivier Henriot, Mathieu Ferland, Audrey-Ann Milot, Tommy Francois, Thomas Paincon, Florent Greffe and Marie-Anne Boutet.
Thanks also to Vladimir Lentzy, Philippe Hédouin, Frédéric Noaro and the rest of the team at Dargaud for their support.

LES DEUX ROYAUMES

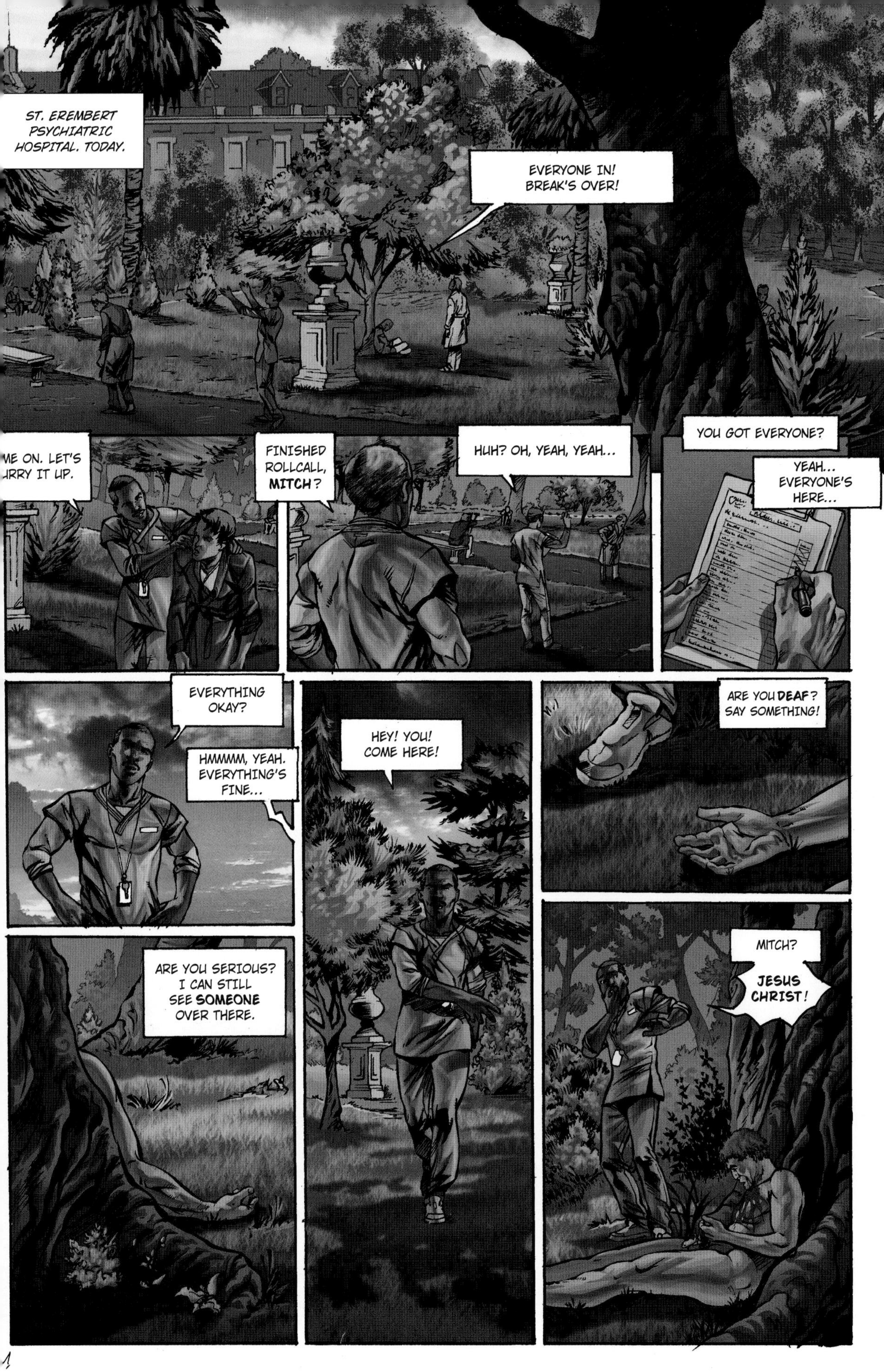
ST. EREMBERT PSYCHIATRIC HOSPITAL. TODAY.
EVERYONE IN! BREAK'S OVER!
ME ON. LET'S
RRY IT UP.
FINISHED ROLLCALL, **MITCH**?
HUH? OH, YEAH, YEAH...
YOU GOT EVERYONE?
YEAH... EVERYONE'S HERE...
EVERYTHING OKAY?
HMMMM, YEAH. EVERYTHING'S FINE...
ARE YOU SERIOUS? I CAN STILL SEE **SOMEONE** OVER THERE.
HEY! YOU! COME HERE!
ARE YOU **DEAF**? SAY SOMETHING!
MITCH?
JESUS CHRIST!

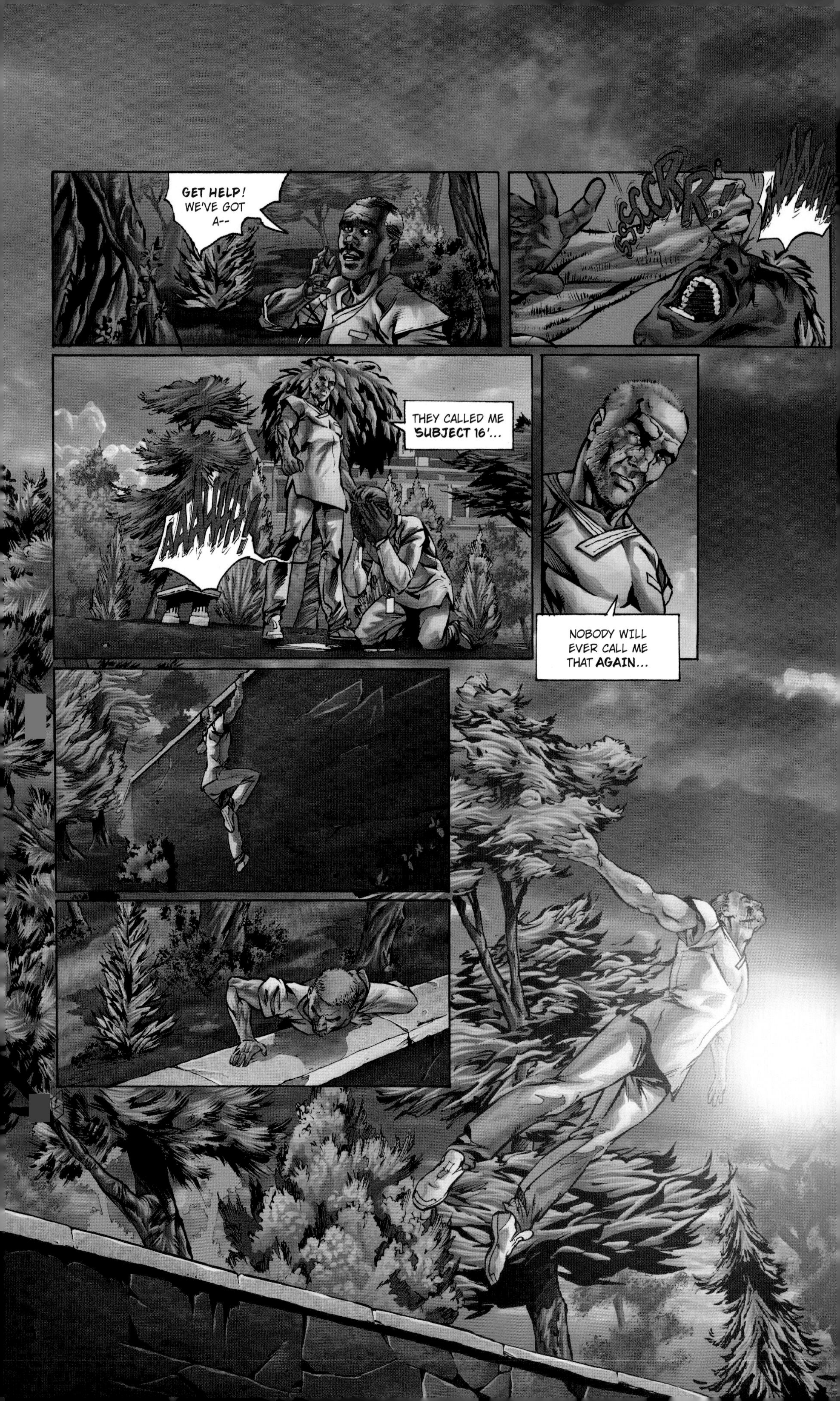

GET HELP! WE'VE GOT A--
SSSCRR!
THEY CALLED ME 'SUBJECT 16'...
AAAHHH!
NOBODY WILL EVER CALL ME THAT AGAIN...

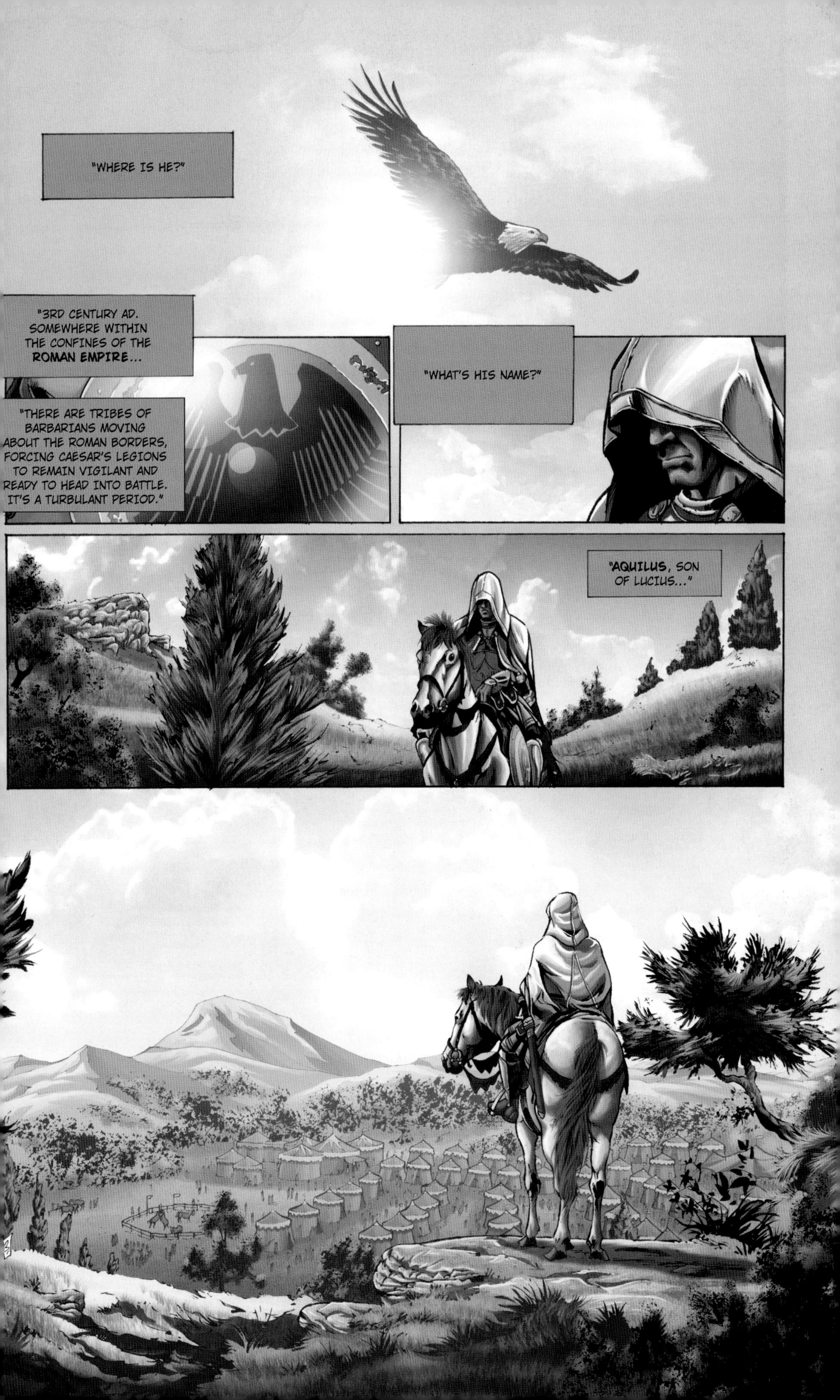
"WHERE IS HE?"
"3RD CENTURY AD. SOMEWHERE WITHIN THE CONFINES OF THE **ROMAN EMPIRE**...
"THERE ARE TRIBES OF BARBARIANS MOVING ABOUT THE ROMAN BORDERS, FORCING CAESAR'S LEGIONS TO REMAIN VIGILANT AND READY TO HEAD INTO BATTLE. IT'S A TURBULANT PERIOD."
"WHAT'S HIS NAME?"
"**AQUILUS**, SON OF LUCIUS..."

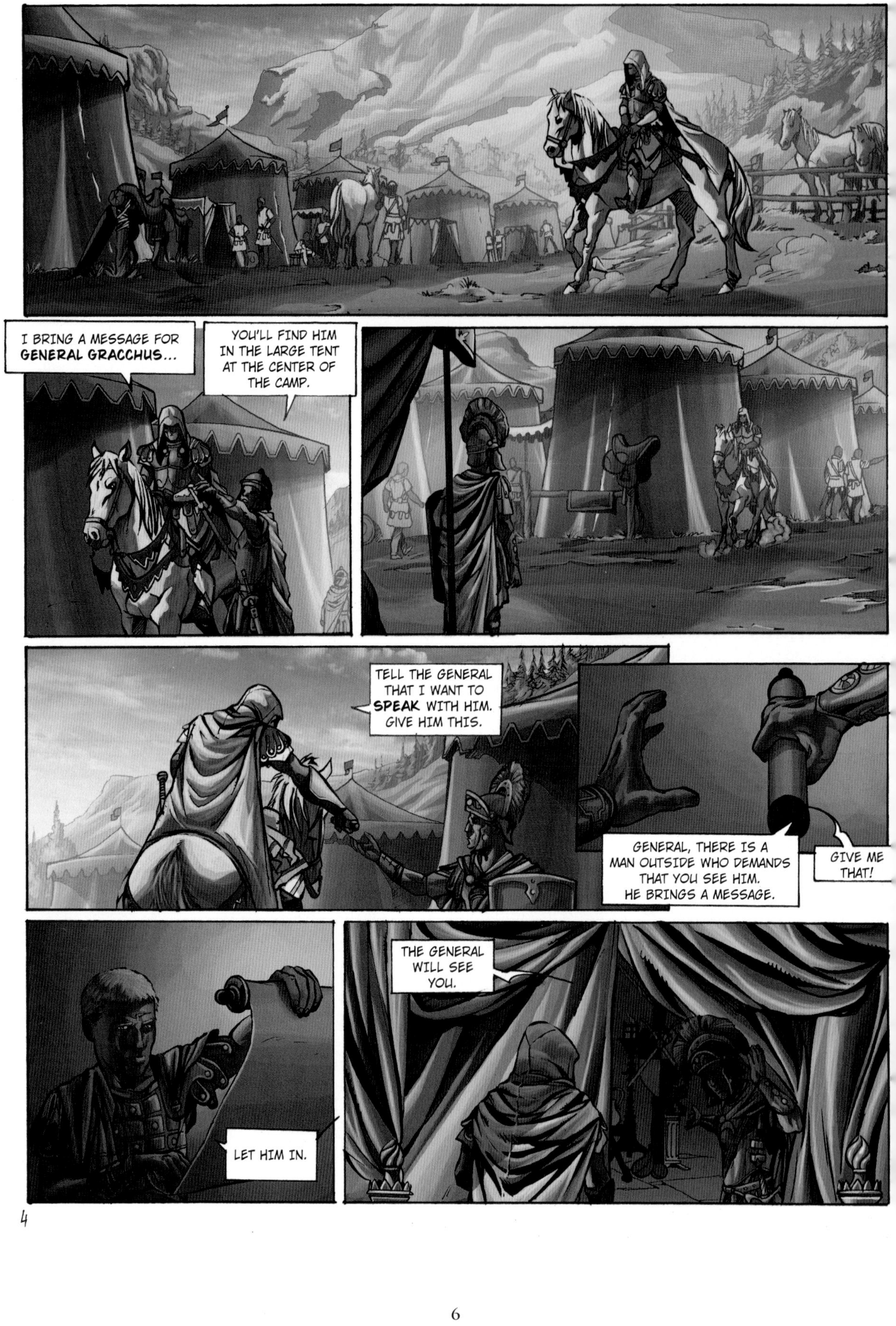
I BRING A MESSAGE FOR GENERAL GRACCHUS...
YOU'LL FIND HIM IN THE LARGE TENT AT THE CENTER OF THE CAMP.
TELL THE GENERAL THAT I WANT TO SPEAK WITH HIM. GIVE HIM THIS.
GENERAL, THERE IS A MAN OUTSIDE WHO DEMANDS THAT YOU SEE HIM. HE BRINGS A MESSAGE.
GIVE ME THAT!
LET HIM IN.
THE GENERAL WILL SEE YOU.
4

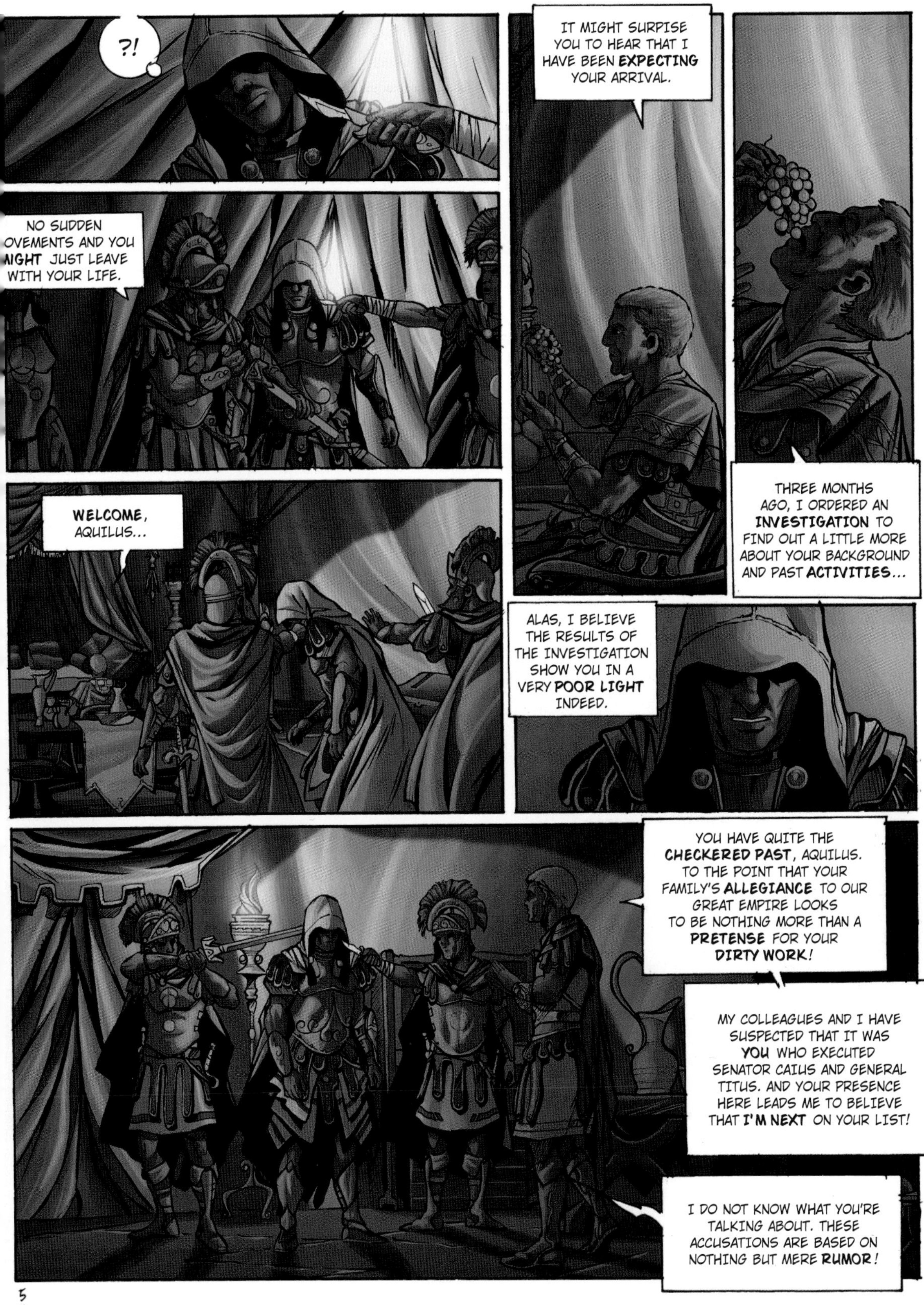
?!
IT MIGHT SURPISE YOU TO HEAR THAT I HAVE BEEN EXPECTING YOUR ARRIVAL.
NO SUDDEN OVEMENTS AND YOU MIGHT JUST LEAVE WITH YOUR LIFE.
THREE MONTHS AGO, I ORDERED AN INVESTIGATION TO FIND OUT A LITTLE MORE ABOUT YOUR BACKGROUND AND PAST ACTIVITIES...
WELCOME, AQUILUS...
ALAS, I BELIEVE THE RESULTS OF THE INVESTIGATION SHOW YOU IN A VERY POOR LIGHT INDEED.
YOU HAVE QUITE THE CHECKERED PAST, AQUILUS. TO THE POINT THAT YOUR FAMILY'S ALLEGIANCE TO OUR GREAT EMPIRE LOOKS TO BE NOTHING MORE THAN A PRETENSE FOR YOUR DIRTY WORK!
MY COLLEAGUES AND I HAVE SUSPECTED THAT IT WAS YOU WHO EXECUTED SENATOR CAIUS AND GENERAL TITUS. AND YOUR PRESENCE HERE LEADS ME TO BELIEVE THAT I'M NEXT ON YOUR LIST!
I DO NOT KNOW WHAT YOU'RE TALKING ABOUT. THESE ACCUSATIONS ARE BASED ON NOTHING BUT MERE RUMOR!

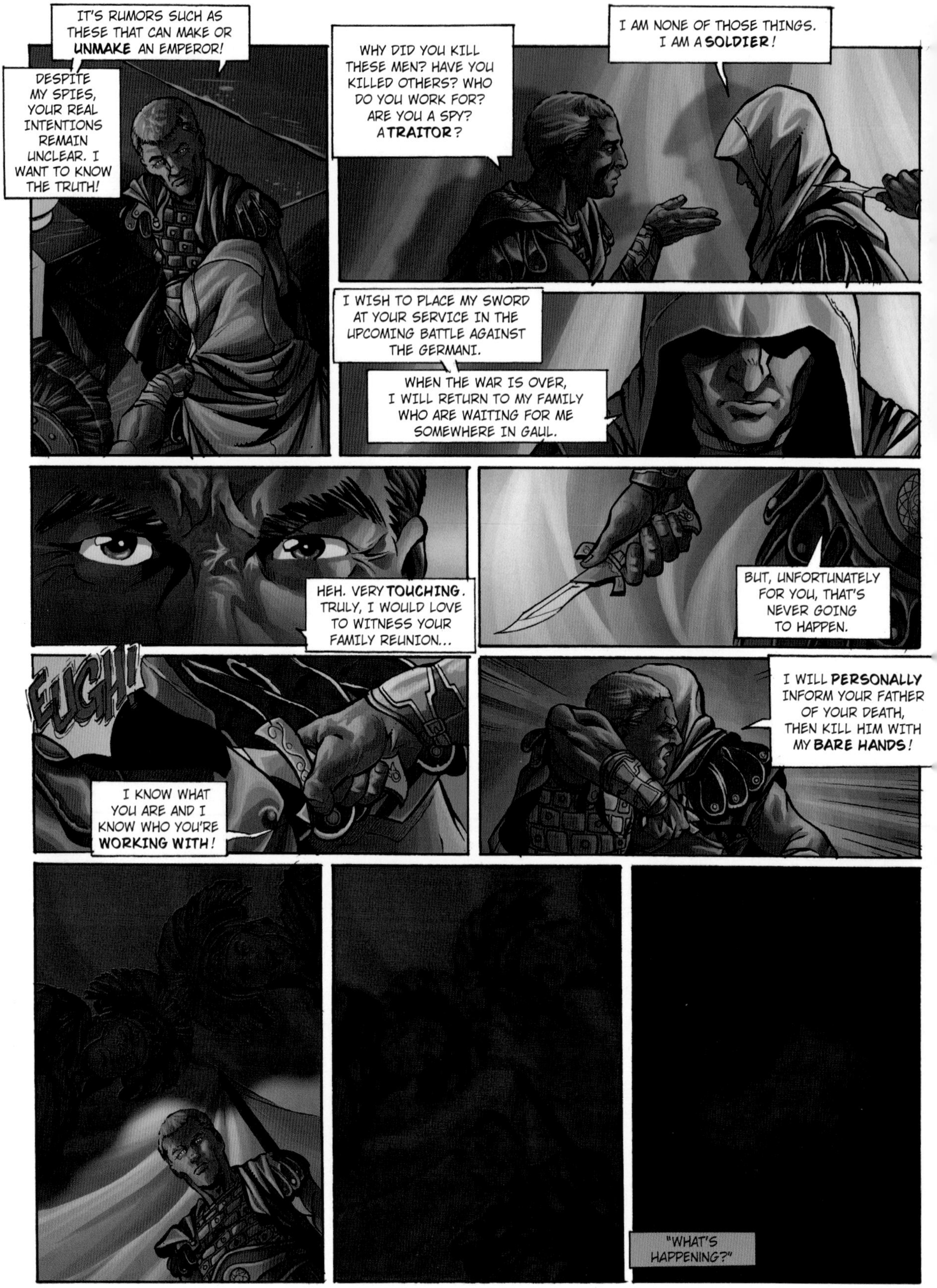
IT'S RUMORS SUCH AS THESE THAT CAN MAKE OR **UNMAKE** AN EMPEROR!
DESPITE MY SPIES, YOUR REAL INTENTIONS REMAIN UNCLEAR. I WANT TO KNOW THE TRUTH!
WHY DID YOU KILL THESE MEN? HAVE YOU KILLED OTHERS? WHO DO YOU WORK FOR? ARE YOU A SPY? A **TRAITOR**?
I AM NONE OF THOSE THINGS. I AM A **SOLDIER**!
I WISH TO PLACE MY SWORD AT YOUR SERVICE IN THE UPCOMING BATTLE AGAINST THE GERMANI.
WHEN THE WAR IS OVER, I WILL RETURN TO MY FAMILY WHO ARE WAITING FOR ME SOMEWHERE IN GAUL.
HEH. VERY **TOUCHING**. TRULY, I WOULD LOVE TO WITNESS YOUR FAMILY REUNION...
BUT, UNFORTUNATELY FOR YOU, THAT'S NEVER GOING TO HAPPEN.
EUGH!
I KNOW WHAT YOU ARE AND I KNOW WHO YOU'RE **WORKING WITH**!
I WILL **PERSONALLY** INFORM YOUR FATHER OF YOUR DEATH, THEN KILL HIM WITH MY **BARE HANDS**!
"WHAT'S HAPPENING?"

6

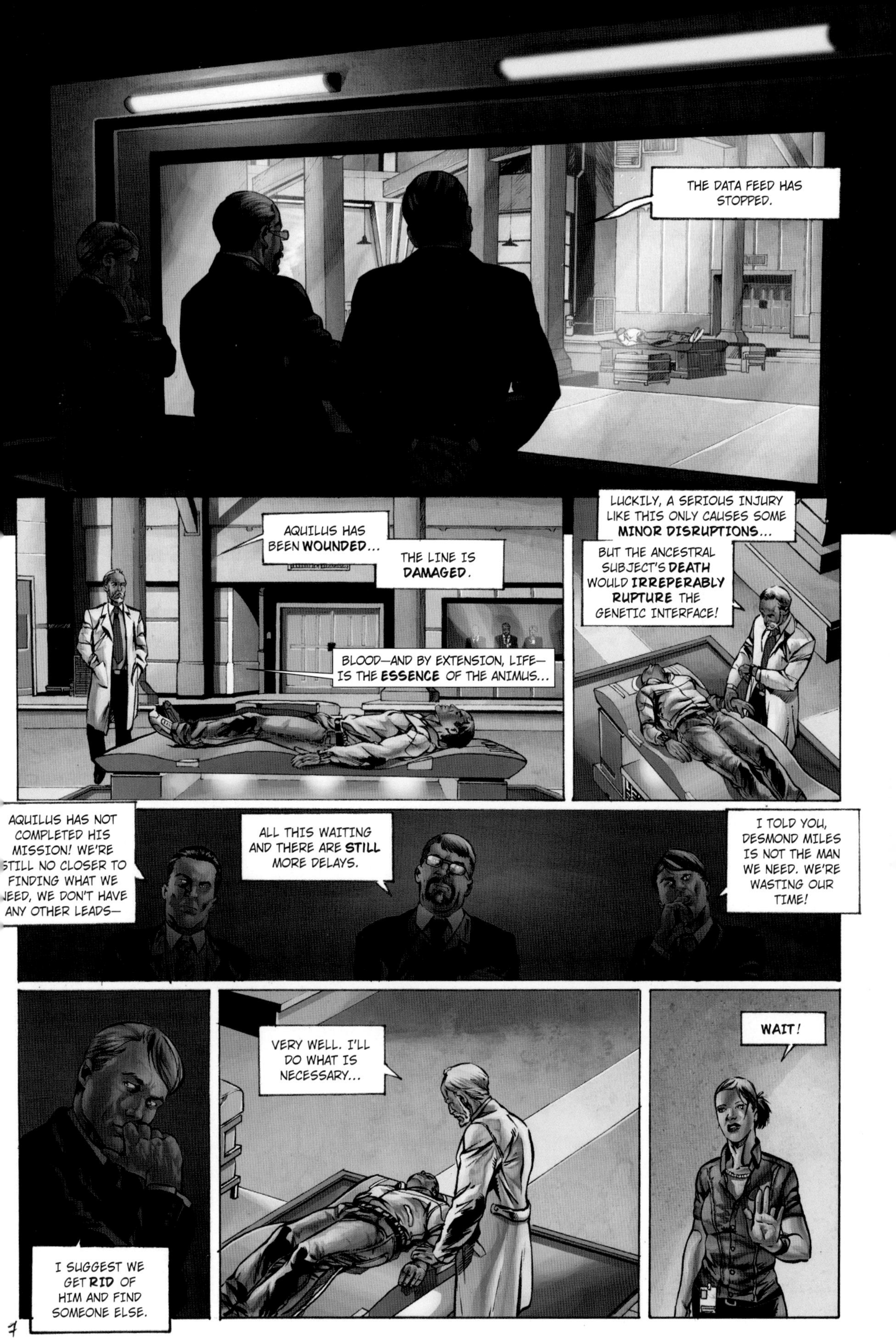
THE DATA FEED HAS STOPPED.
AQUILUS HAS BEEN WOUNDED...
THE LINE IS DAMAGED.
BLOOD—AND BY EXTENSION, LIFE—IS THE ESSENCE OF THE ANIMUS...
LUCKILY, A SERIOUS INJURY LIKE THIS ONLY CAUSES SOME MINOR DISRUPTIONS...
BUT THE ANCESTRAL SUBJECT'S DEATH WOULD IRREPERABLY RUPTURE THE GENETIC INTERFACE!
AQUILUS HAS NOT COMPLETED HIS MISSION! WE'RE STILL NO CLOSER TO FINDING WHAT WE NEED, WE DON'T HAVE ANY OTHER LEADS—
ALL THIS WAITING AND THERE ARE STILL MORE DELAYS.
I TOLD YOU, DESMOND MILES IS NOT THE MAN WE NEED. WE'RE WASTING OUR TIME!
I SUGGEST WE GET RID OF HIM AND FIND SOMEONE ELSE.
VERY WELL. I'LL DO WHAT IS NECESSARY...
WAIT!

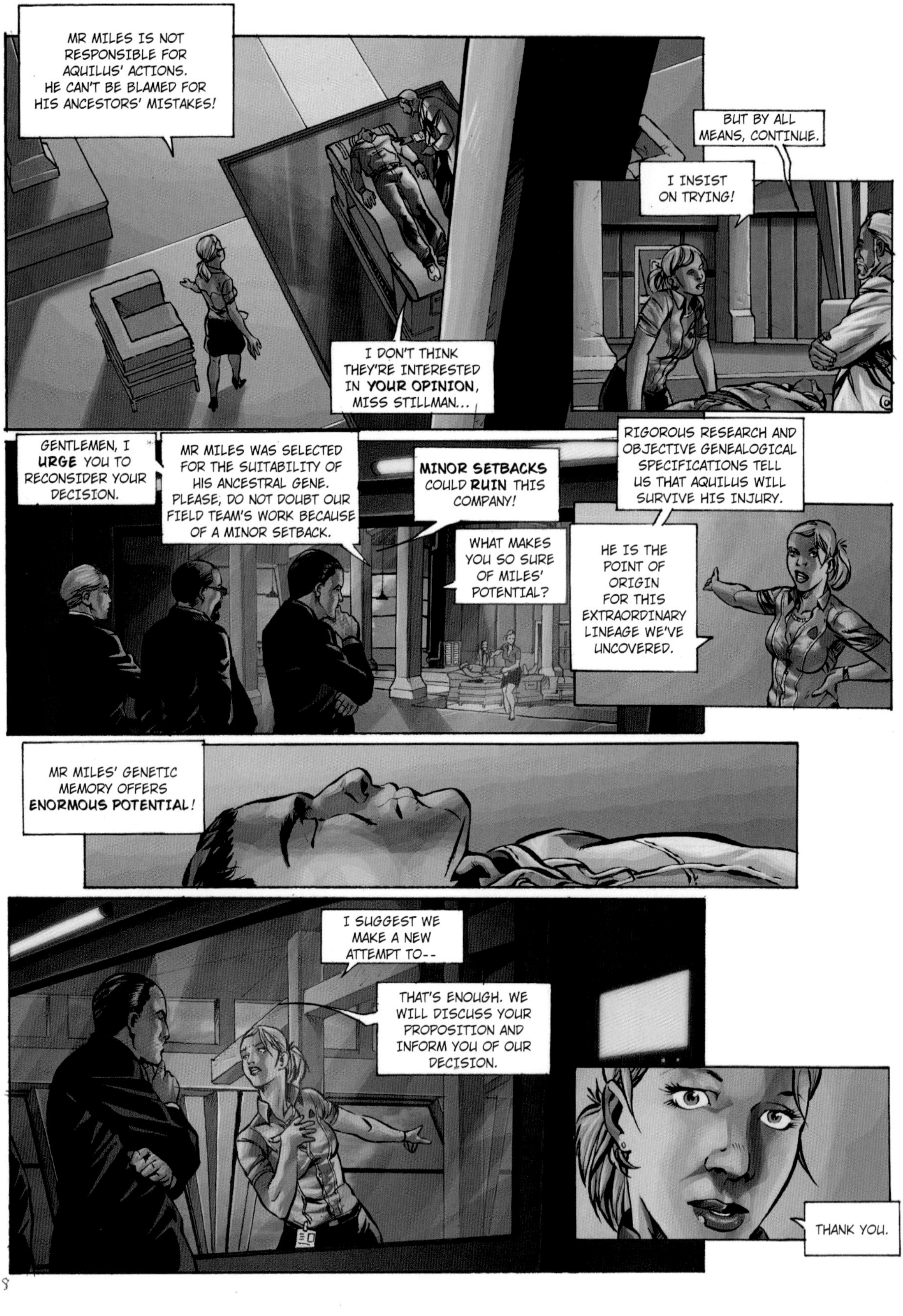
MR MILES IS NOT RESPONSIBLE FOR AQUILUS' ACTIONS. HE CAN'T BE BLAMED FOR HIS ANCESTORS' MISTAKES!
I DON'T THINK THEY'RE INTERESTED IN **YOUR OPINION**, MISS STILLMAN...
I INSIST ON TRYING!
BUT BY ALL MEANS, CONTINUE.
GENTLEMEN, I **URGE** YOU TO RECONSIDER YOUR DECISION.
MR MILES WAS SELECTED FOR THE SUITABILITY OF HIS ANCESTRAL GENE. PLEASE, DO NOT DOUBT OUR FIELD TEAM'S WORK BECAUSE OF A MINOR SETBACK.
MINOR SETBACKS COULD **RUIN** THIS COMPANY!
WHAT MAKES YOU SO SURE OF MILES' POTENTIAL?
RIGOROUS RESEARCH AND OBJECTIVE GENEALOGICAL SPECIFICATIONS TELL US THAT AQUILUS WILL SURVIVE HIS INJURY.
HE IS THE POINT OF ORIGIN FOR THIS EXTRAORDINARY LINEAGE WE'VE UNCOVERED.
MR MILES' GENETIC MEMORY OFFERS **ENORMOUS POTENTIAL**!
I SUGGEST WE MAKE A NEW ATTEMPT TO--
THAT'S ENOUGH. WE WILL DISCUSS YOUR PROPOSITION AND INFORM YOU OF OUR DECISION.
THANK YOU.

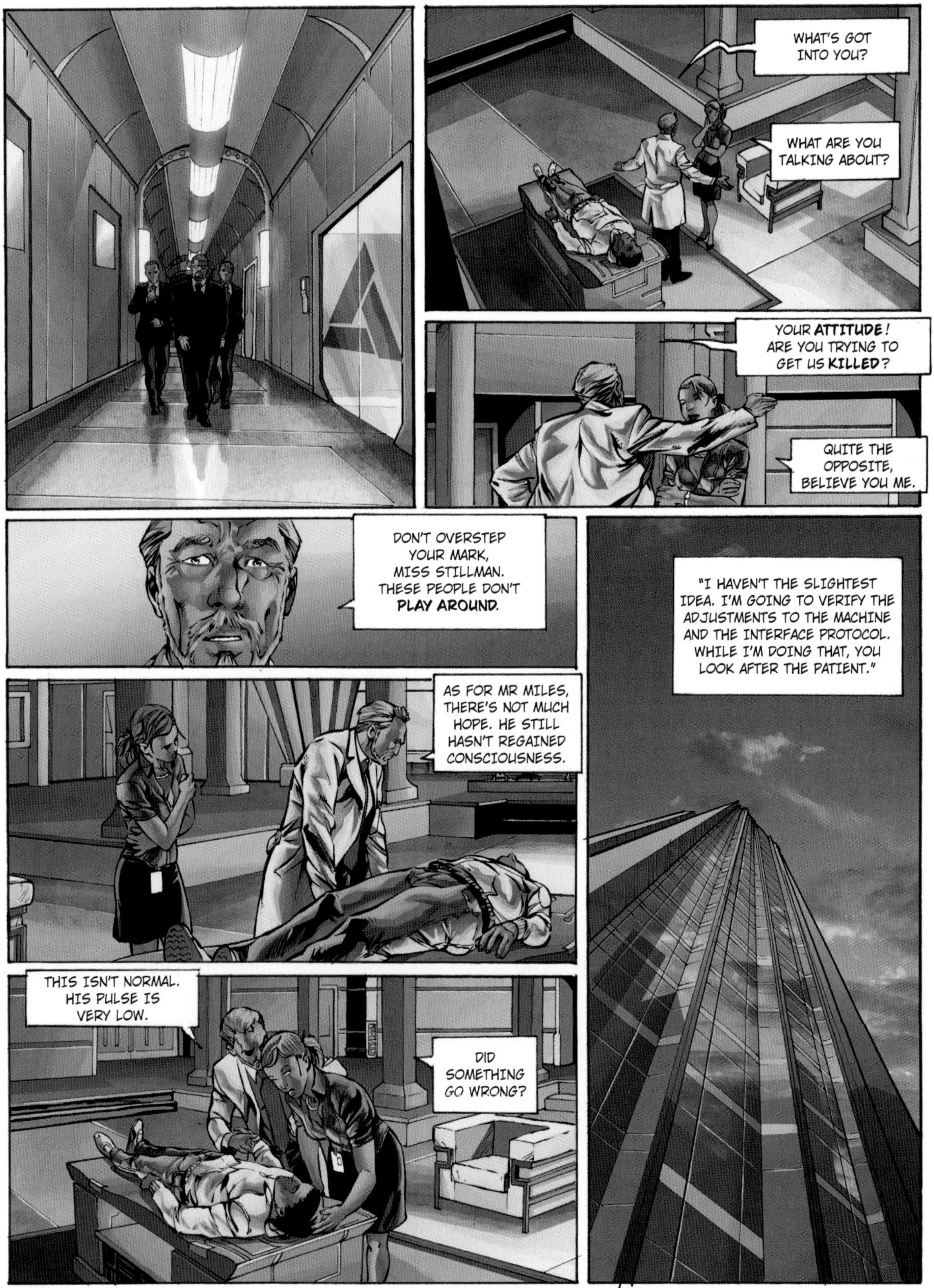
WHAT'S GOT INTO YOU?
WHAT ARE YOU TALKING ABOUT?
YOUR ATTITUDE! ARE YOU TRYING TO GET US KILLED?
QUITE THE OPPOSITE, BELIEVE YOU ME.
DON'T OVERSTEP YOUR MARK, MISS STILLMAN. THESE PEOPLE DON'T PLAY AROUND.
"I HAVEN'T THE SLIGHTEST IDEA. I'M GOING TO VERIFY THE ADJUSTMENTS TO THE MACHINE AND THE INTERFACE PROTOCOL. WHILE I'M DOING THAT, YOU LOOK AFTER THE PATIENT."
AS FOR MR MILES, THERE'S NOT MUCH HOPE. HE STILL HASN'T REGAINED CONSCIOUSNESS.
THIS ISN'T NORMAL. HIS PULSE IS VERY LOW.
DID SOMETHING GO WRONG?

9

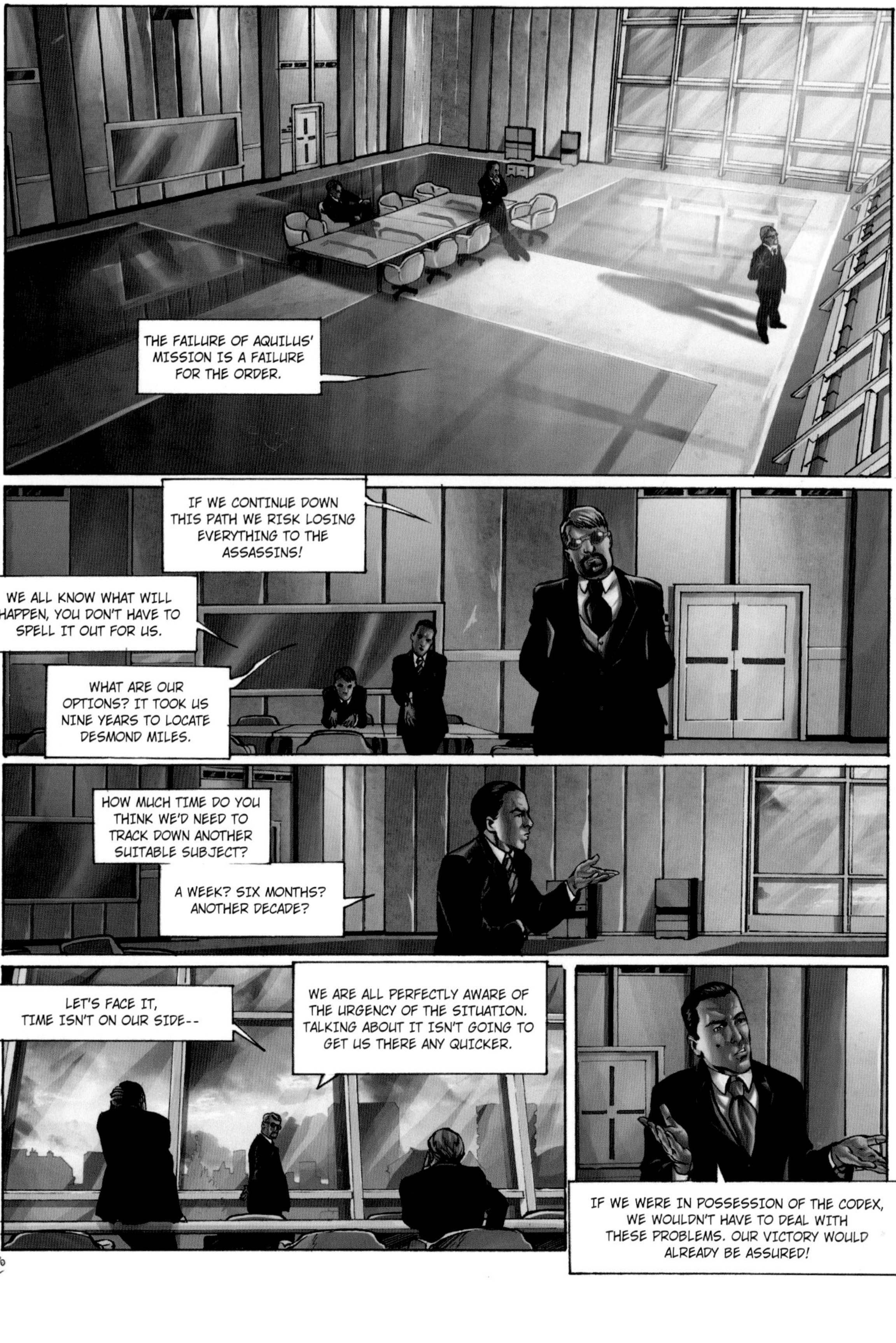
THE FAILURE OF AQUILUS' MISSION IS A FAILURE FOR THE ORDER.
IF WE CONTINUE DOWN THIS PATH WE RISK LOSING EVERYTHING TO THE ASSASSINS!
WE ALL KNOW WHAT WILL HAPPEN, YOU DON'T HAVE TO SPELL IT OUT FOR US.
WHAT ARE OUR OPTIONS? IT TOOK US NINE YEARS TO LOCATE DESMOND MILES.
HOW MUCH TIME DO YOU THINK WE'D NEED TO TRACK DOWN ANOTHER SUITABLE SUBJECT?
A WEEK? SIX MONTHS? ANOTHER DECADE?
LET'S FACE IT, TIME ISN'T ON OUR SIDE--
WE ARE ALL PERFECTLY AWARE OF THE URGENCY OF THE SITUATION. TALKING ABOUT IT ISN'T GOING TO GET US THERE ANY QUICKER.
IF WE WERE IN POSSESSION OF THE CODEX, WE WOULDN'T HAVE TO DEAL WITH THESE PROBLEMS. OUR VICTORY WOULD ALREADY BE ASSURED!

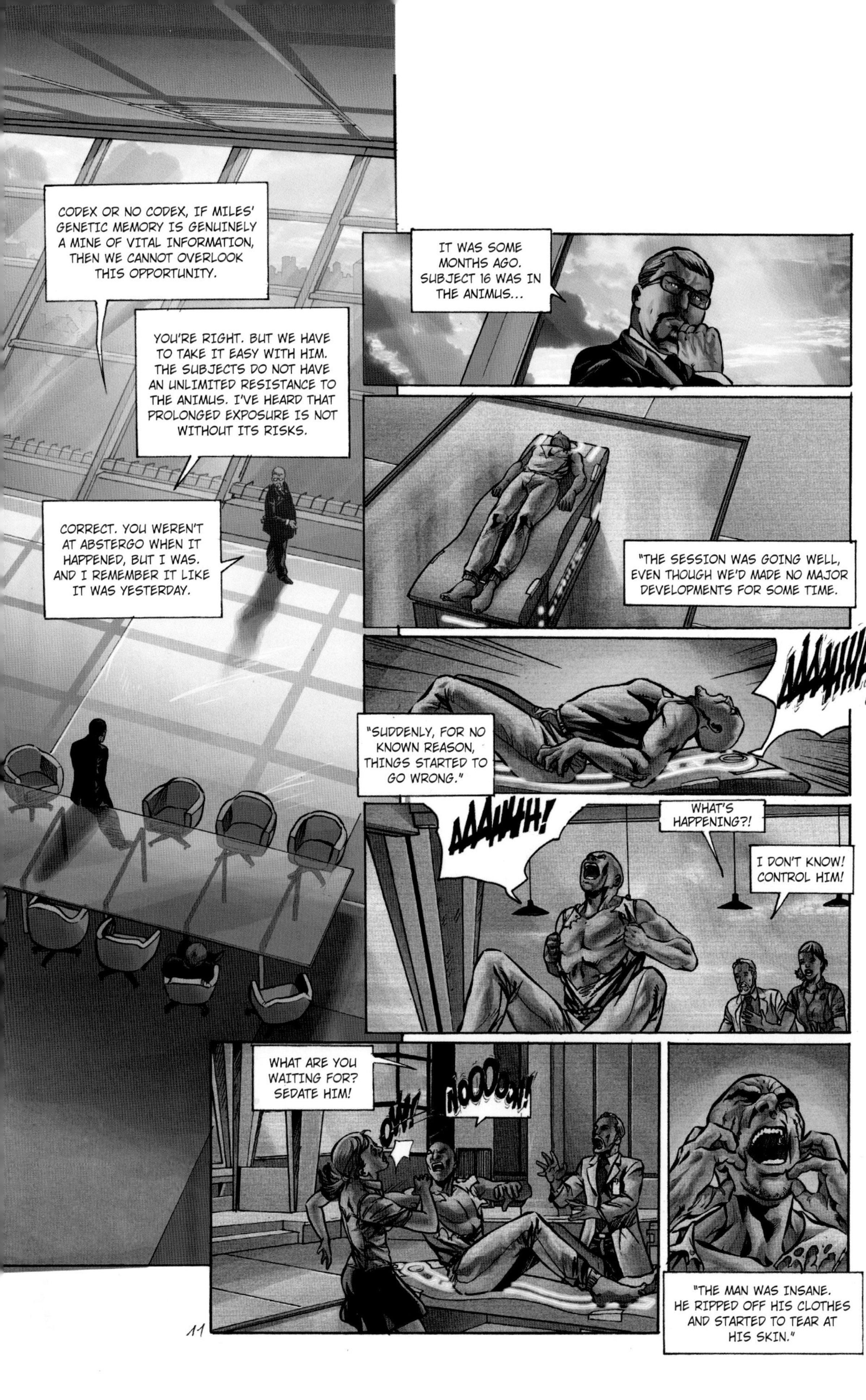
CODEX OR NO CODEX, IF MILES' GENETIC MEMORY IS GENUINELY A MINE OF VITAL INFORMATION, THEN WE CANNOT OVERLOOK THIS OPPORTUNITY.
YOU'RE RIGHT. BUT WE HAVE TO TAKE IT EASY WITH HIM. THE SUBJECTS DO NOT HAVE AN UNLIMITED RESISTANCE TO THE ANIMUS. I'VE HEARD THAT PROLONGED EXPOSURE IS NOT WITHOUT ITS RISKS.
CORRECT. YOU WEREN'T AT ABSTERGO WHEN IT HAPPENED, BUT I WAS. AND I REMEMBER IT LIKE IT WAS YESTERDAY.
IT WAS SOME MONTHS AGO. SUBJECT 16 WAS IN THE ANIMUS...
"THE SESSION WAS GOING WELL, EVEN THOUGH WE'D MADE NO MAJOR DEVELOPMENTS FOR SOME TIME.
"SUDDENLY, FOR NO KNOWN REASON, THINGS STARTED TO GO WRONG."
AAAHHH!
AAAHHH!
WHAT'S HAPPENING?!
I DON'T KNOW! CONTROL HIM!
WHAT ARE YOU WAITING FOR? SEDATE HIM!
OW!
NOOOOOH!
"THE MAN WAS INSANE. HE RIPPED OFF HIS CLOTHES AND STARTED TO TEAR AT HIS SKIN."
11

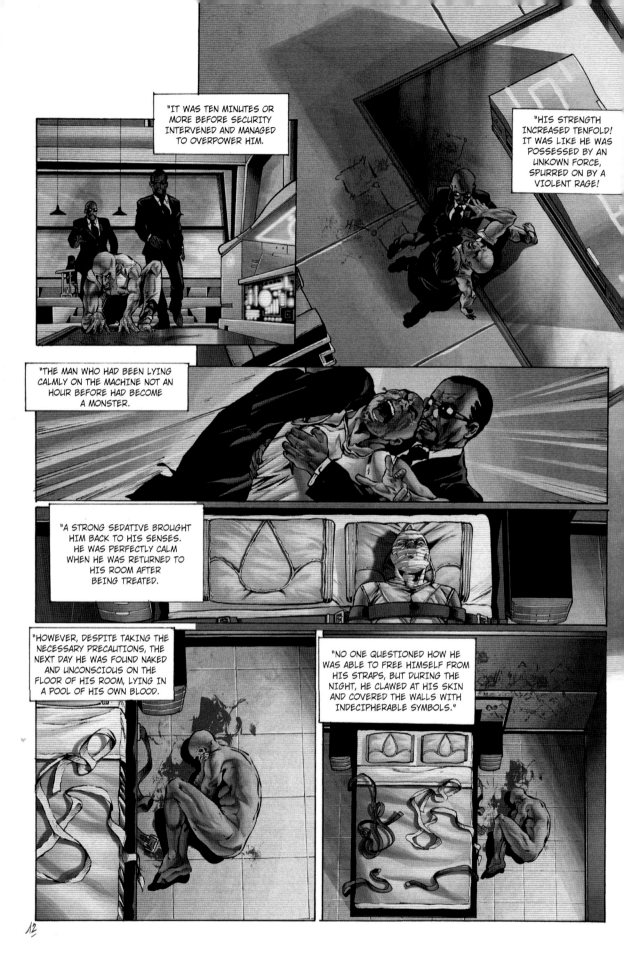

"IT WAS TEN MINUTES OR MORE BEFORE SECURITY INTERVENED AND MANAGED TO OVERPOWER HIM.

"HIS STRENGTH INCREASED TENFOLD! IT WAS LIKE HE WAS POSSESSED BY AN UNKOWN FORCE, SPURRED ON BY A VIOLENT RAGE!

"THE MAN WHO HAD BEEN LYING CALMLY ON THE MACHINE NOT AN HOUR BEFORE HAD BECOME A MONSTER.

"A STRONG SEDATIVE BROUGHT HIM BACK TO HIS SENSES. HE WAS PERFECTLY CALM WHEN HE WAS RETURNED TO HIS ROOM AFTER BEING TREATED.

"HOWEVER, DESPITE TAKING THE NECESSARY PRECAUTIONS, THE NEXT DAY HE WAS FOUND NAKED AND UNCONSCIOUS ON THE FLOOR OF HIS ROOM, LYING IN A POOL OF HIS OWN BLOOD.

"NO ONE QUESTIONED HOW HE WAS ABLE TO FREE HIMSELF FROM HIS STRAPS, BUT DURING THE NIGHT, HE CLAWED AT HIS SKIN AND COVERED THE WALLS WITH INDECIPHERABLE SYMBOLS."

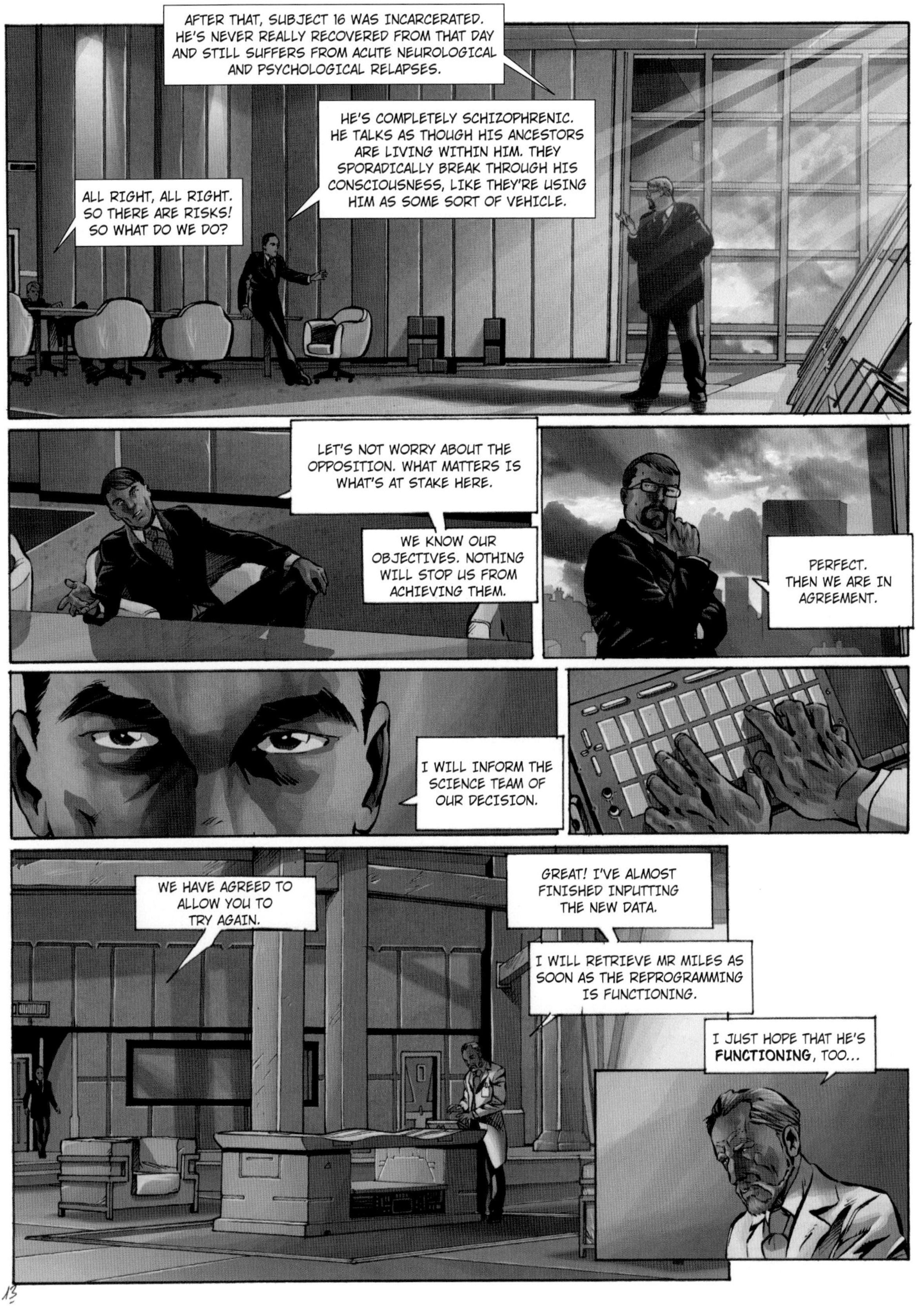
AFTER THAT, SUBJECT 16 WAS INCARCERATED. HE'S NEVER REALLY RECOVERED FROM THAT DAY AND STILL SUFFERS FROM ACUTE NEUROLOGICAL AND PSYCHOLOGICAL RELAPSES.
HE'S COMPLETELY SCHIZOPHRENIC. HE TALKS AS THOUGH HIS ANCESTORS ARE LIVING WITHIN HIM. THEY SPORADICALLY BREAK THROUGH HIS CONSCIOUSNESS, LIKE THEY'RE USING HIM AS SOME SORT OF VEHICLE.
ALL RIGHT, ALL RIGHT. SO THERE ARE RISKS! SO WHAT DO WE DO?
LET'S NOT WORRY ABOUT THE OPPOSITION. WHAT MATTERS IS WHAT'S AT STAKE HERE.
WE KNOW OUR OBJECTIVES. NOTHING WILL STOP US FROM ACHIEVING THEM.
PERFECT. THEN WE ARE IN AGREEMENT.
I WILL INFORM THE SCIENCE TEAM OF OUR DECISION.
WE HAVE AGREED TO ALLOW YOU TO TRY AGAIN.
GREAT! I'VE ALMOST FINISHED INPUTTING THE NEW DATA.
I WILL RETRIEVE MR MILES AS SOON AS THE REPROGRAMMING IS FUNCTIONING.
I JUST HOPE THAT HE'S **FUNCTIONING**, TOO...
13

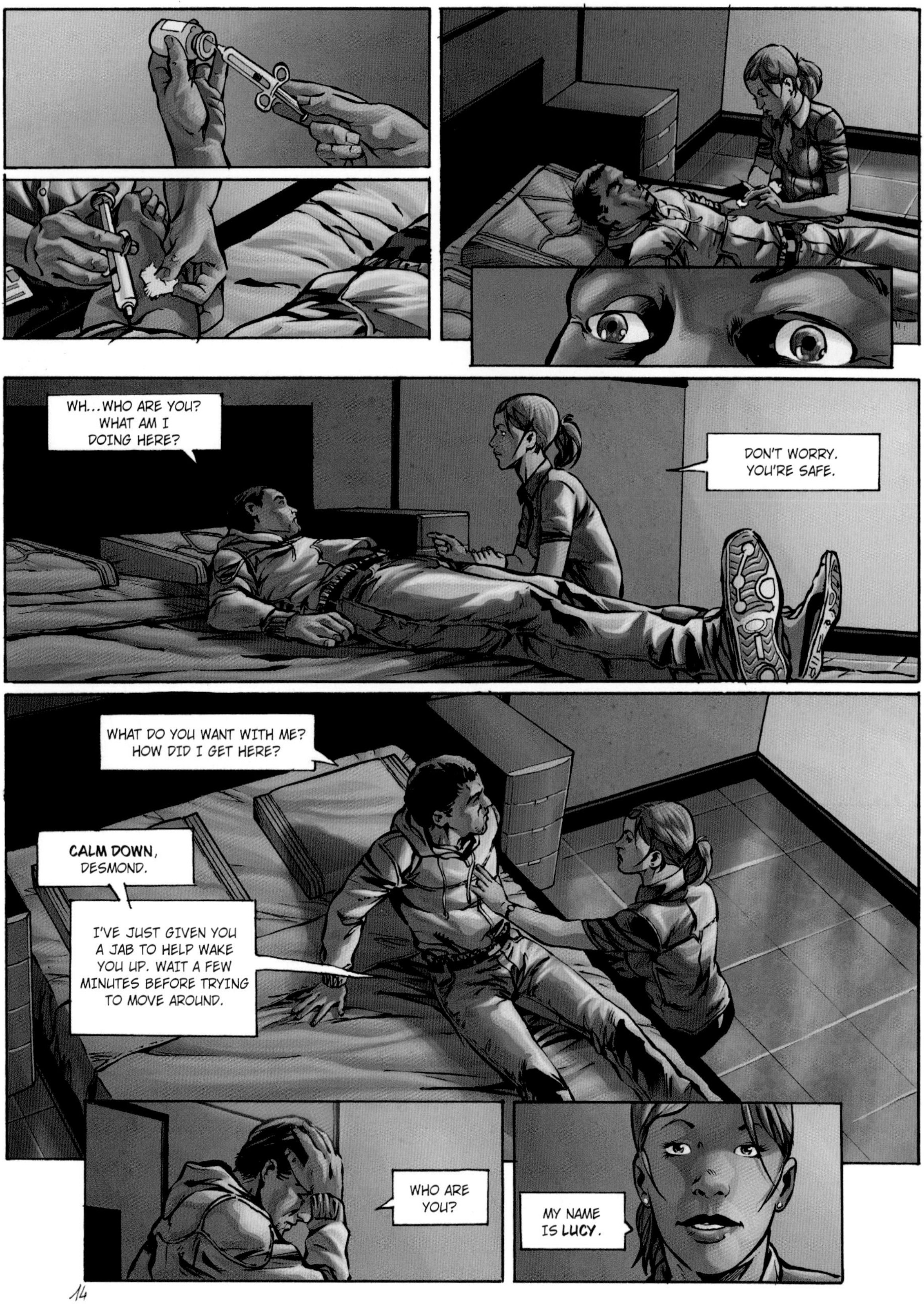

WH...WHO ARE YOU? WHAT AM I DOING HERE?
DON'T WORRY. YOU'RE SAFE.
WHAT DO YOU WANT WITH ME? HOW DID I GET HERE?
CALM DOWN, DESMOND.
I'VE JUST GIVEN YOU A JAB TO HELP WAKE YOU UP. WAIT A FEW MINUTES BEFORE TRYING TO MOVE AROUND.
WHO ARE YOU?
MY NAME IS LUCY.
14

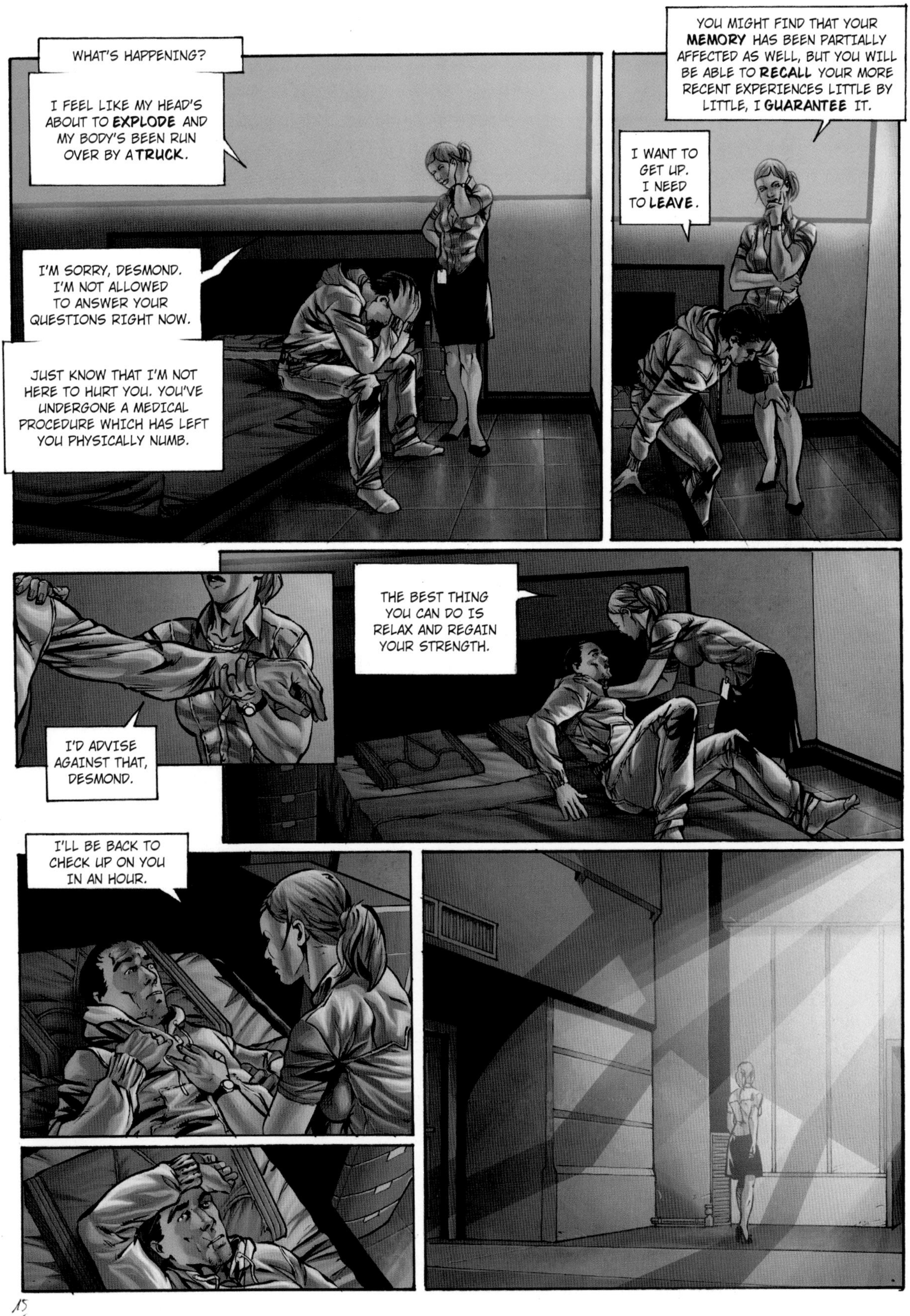
WHAT'S HAPPENING?
I FEEL LIKE MY HEAD'S ABOUT TO EXPLODE AND MY BODY'S BEEN RUN OVER BY A TRUCK.
I'M SORRY, DESMOND. I'M NOT ALLOWED TO ANSWER YOUR QUESTIONS RIGHT NOW.
JUST KNOW THAT I'M NOT HERE TO HURT YOU. YOU'VE UNDERGONE A MEDICAL PROCEDURE WHICH HAS LEFT YOU PHYSICALLY NUMB.
YOU MIGHT FIND THAT YOUR MEMORY HAS BEEN PARTIALLY AFFECTED AS WELL, BUT YOU WILL BE ABLE TO RECALL YOUR MORE RECENT EXPERIENCES LITTLE BY LITTLE, I GUARANTEE IT.
I WANT TO GET UP. I NEED TO LEAVE.
I'D ADVISE AGAINST THAT, DESMOND.
THE BEST THING YOU CAN DO IS RELAX AND REGAIN YOUR STRENGTH.
I'LL BE BACK TO CHECK UP ON YOU IN AN HOUR.
15

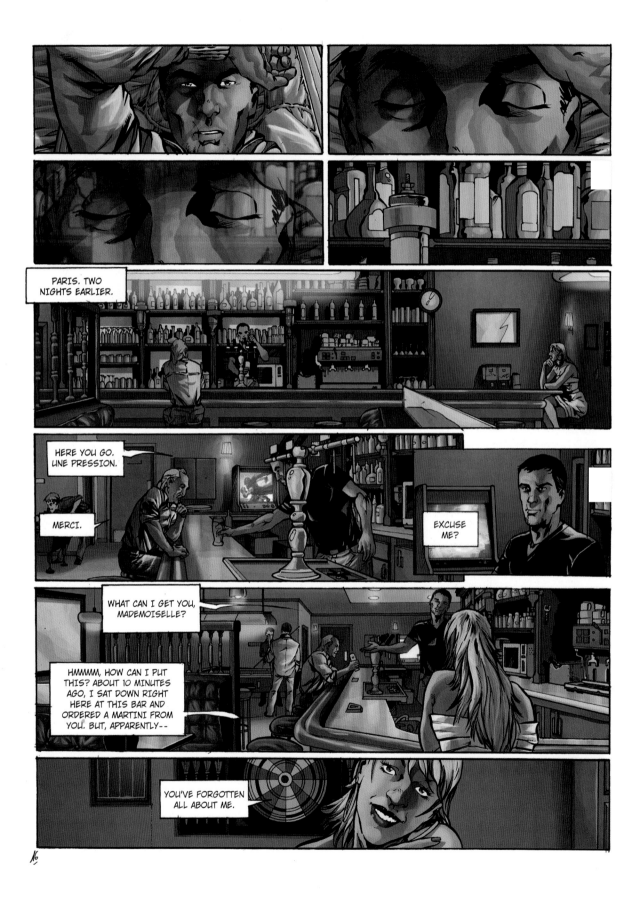

PARIS. TWO NIGHTS EARLIER.

HERE YOU GO. UNE PRESSION.

MERCI.

EXCUSE ME?

WHAT CAN I GET YOU, MADEMOISELLE?

HMMMM, HOW CAN I PUT THIS? ABOUT 10 MINUTES AGO, I SAT DOWN RIGHT HERE AT THIS BAR AND ORDERED A MARTINI FROM YOU. BUT, APPARENTLY--

YOU'VE FORGOTTEN ALL ABOUT ME.

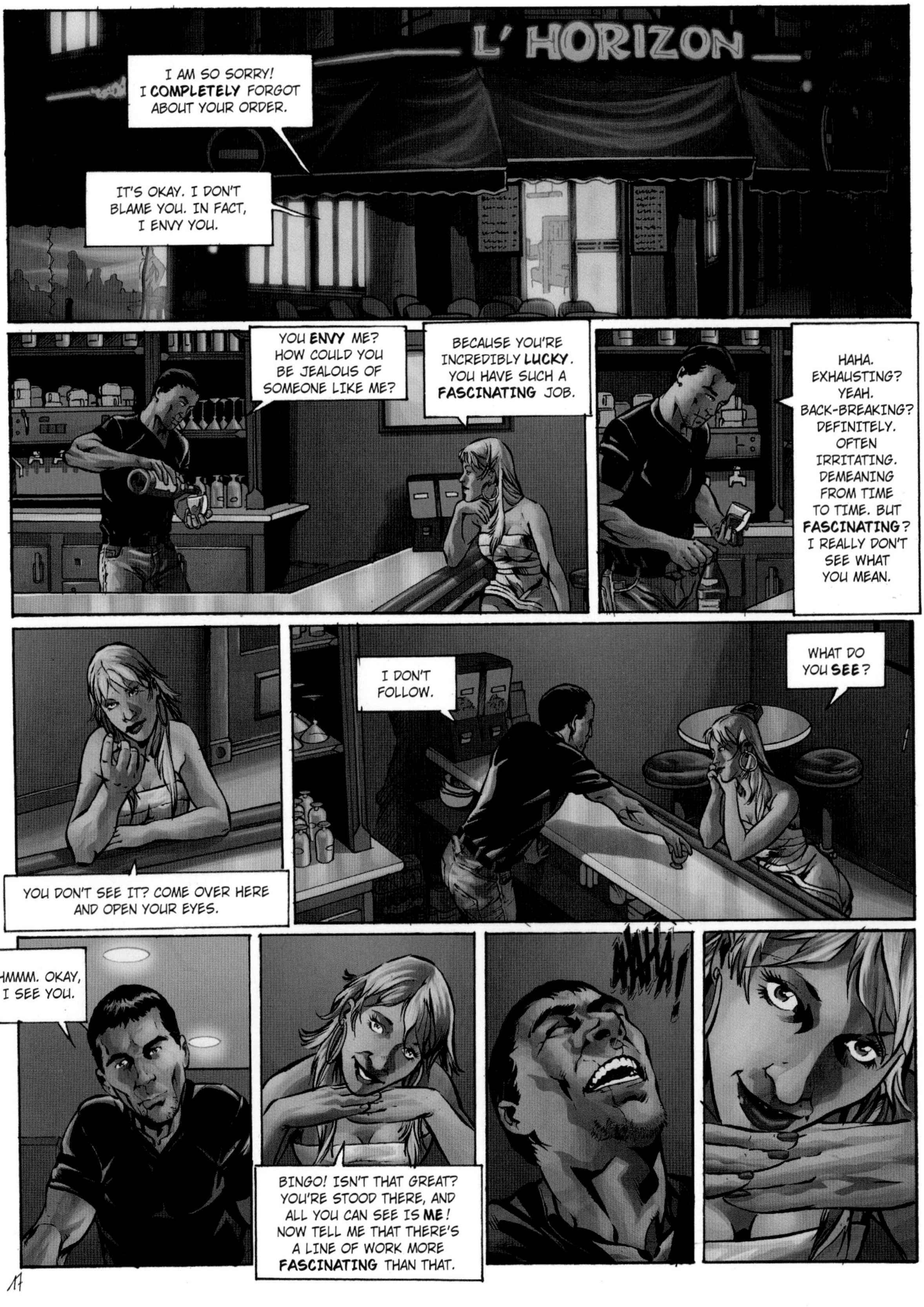
L' HORIZON
I AM SO SORRY! I COMPLETELY FORGOT ABOUT YOUR ORDER.
IT'S OKAY. I DON'T BLAME YOU. IN FACT, I ENVY YOU.
YOU ENVY ME? HOW COULD YOU BE JEALOUS OF SOMEONE LIKE ME?
BECAUSE YOU'RE INCREDIBLY LUCKY. YOU HAVE SUCH A FASCINATING JOB.
HAHA. EXHAUSTING? YEAH. BACK-BREAKING? DEFINITELY. OFTEN IRRITATING. DEMEANING FROM TIME TO TIME. BUT FASCINATING? I REALLY DON'T SEE WHAT YOU MEAN.
YOU DON'T SEE IT? COME OVER HERE AND OPEN YOUR EYES.
I DON'T FOLLOW.
WHAT DO YOU SEE?
HMMM. OKAY, I SEE YOU.
BINGO! ISN'T THAT GREAT? YOU'RE STOOD THERE, AND ALL YOU CAN SEE IS ME! NOW TELL ME THAT THERE'S A LINE OF WORK MORE FASCINATING THAN THAT.
AHAHA!
17

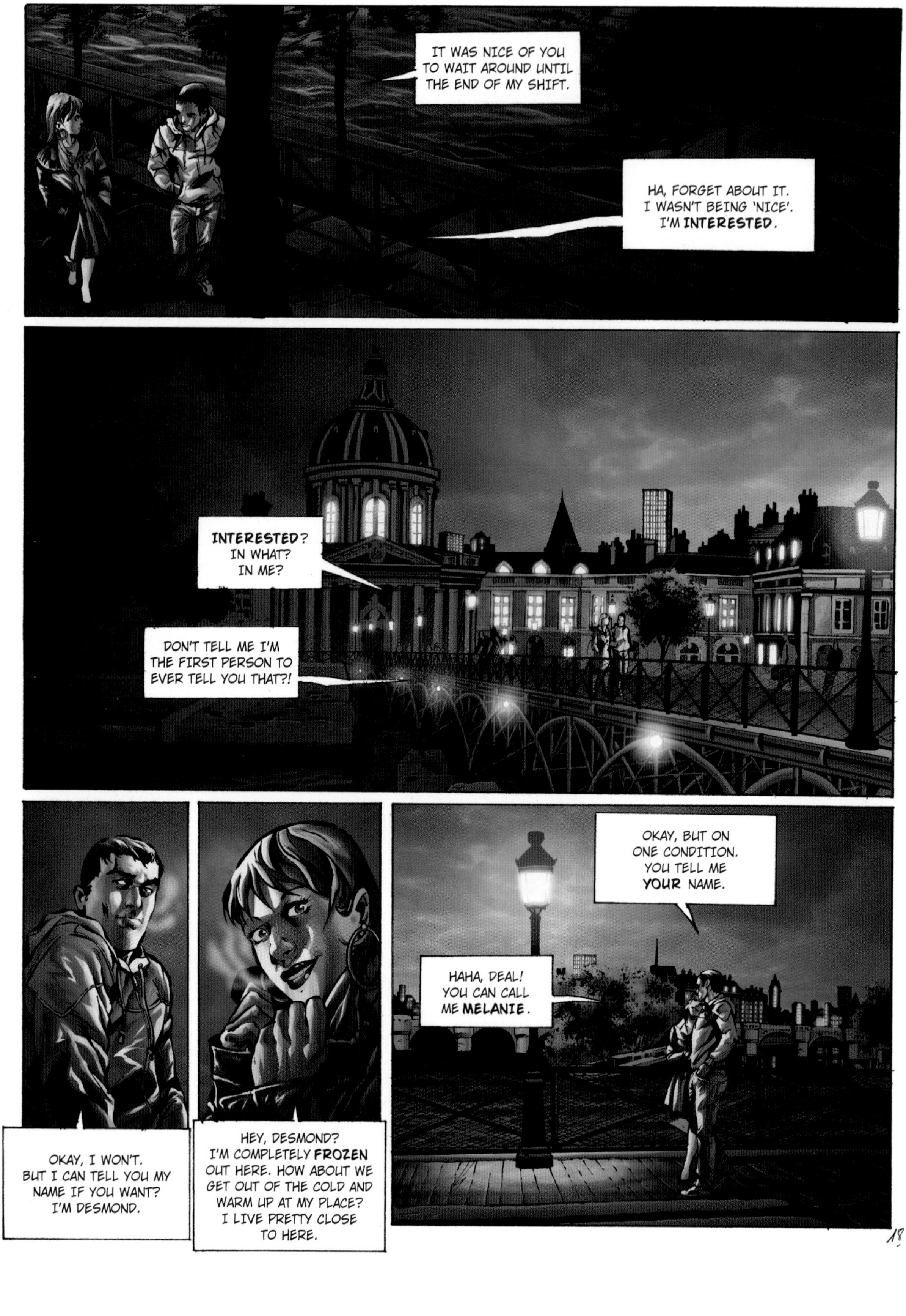
IT WAS NICE OF YOU TO WAIT AROUND UNTIL THE END OF MY SHIFT.
HA, FORGET ABOUT IT. I WASN'T BEING 'NICE'. I'M **INTERESTED**.
INTERESTED? IN WHAT? IN ME?
DON'T TELL ME I'M THE FIRST PERSON TO EVER TELL YOU THAT?!
OKAY, I WON'T. BUT I CAN TELL YOU MY NAME IF YOU WANT? I'M DESMOND.
HEY, DESMOND? I'M COMPLETELY **FROZEN** OUT HERE. HOW ABOUT WE GET OUT OF THE COLD AND WARM UP AT MY PLACE? I LIVE PRETTY CLOSE TO HERE.
OKAY, BUT ON ONE CONDITION. YOU TELL ME **YOUR** NAME.
HAHA, DEAL! YOU CAN CALL ME **MELANIE**.
18

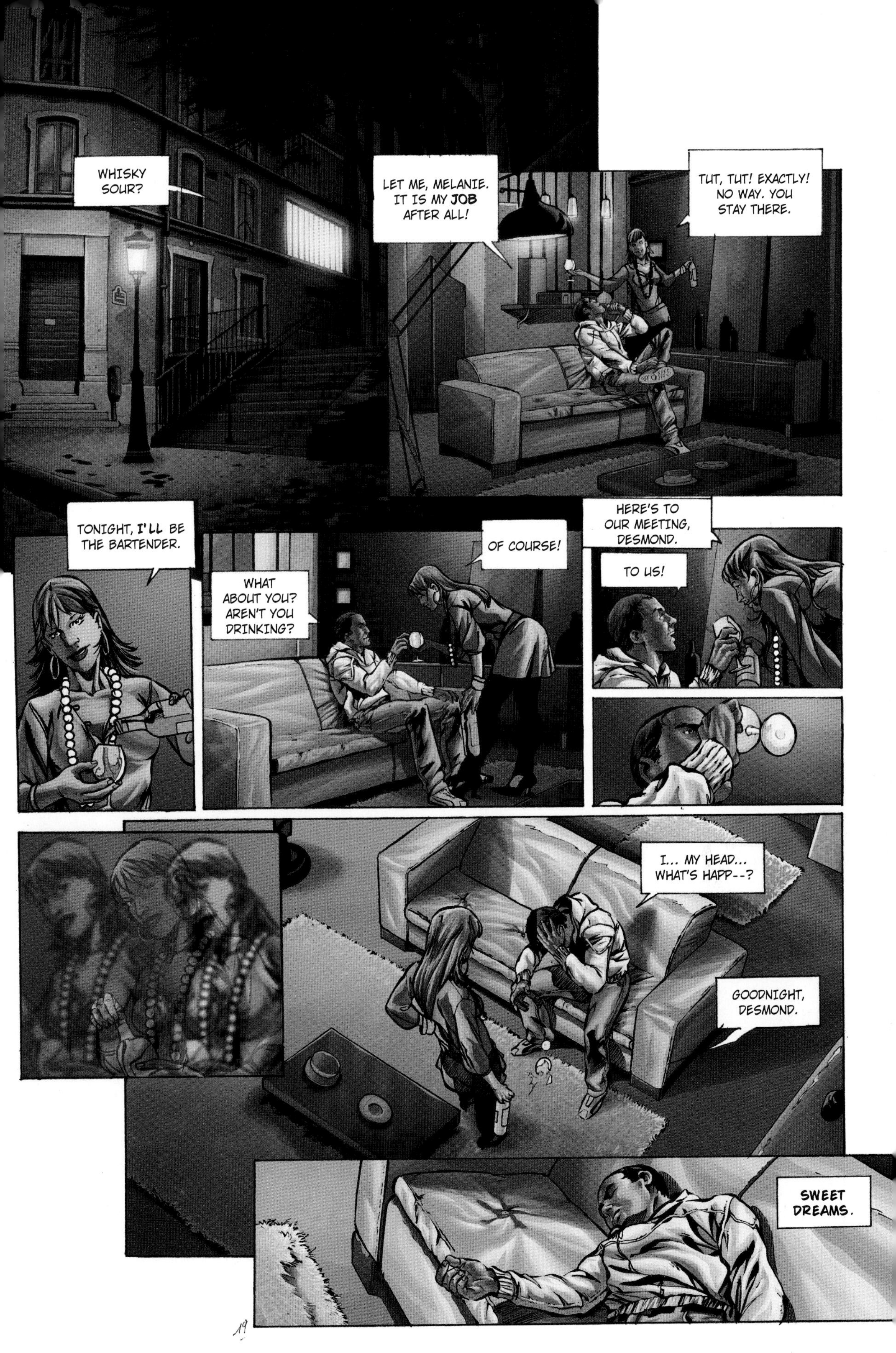
WHISKY SOUR?
LET ME, MELANIE. IT IS MY JOB AFTER ALL!
TUT, TUT! EXACTLY! NO WAY. YOU STAY THERE.
TONIGHT, I'LL BE THE BARTENDER.
OF COURSE!
WHAT ABOUT YOU? AREN'T YOU DRINKING?
HERE'S TO OUR MEETING, DESMOND.
TO US!
I... MY HEAD... WHAT'S HAPP--?
GOODNIGHT, DESMOND.
SWEET DREAMS.
19

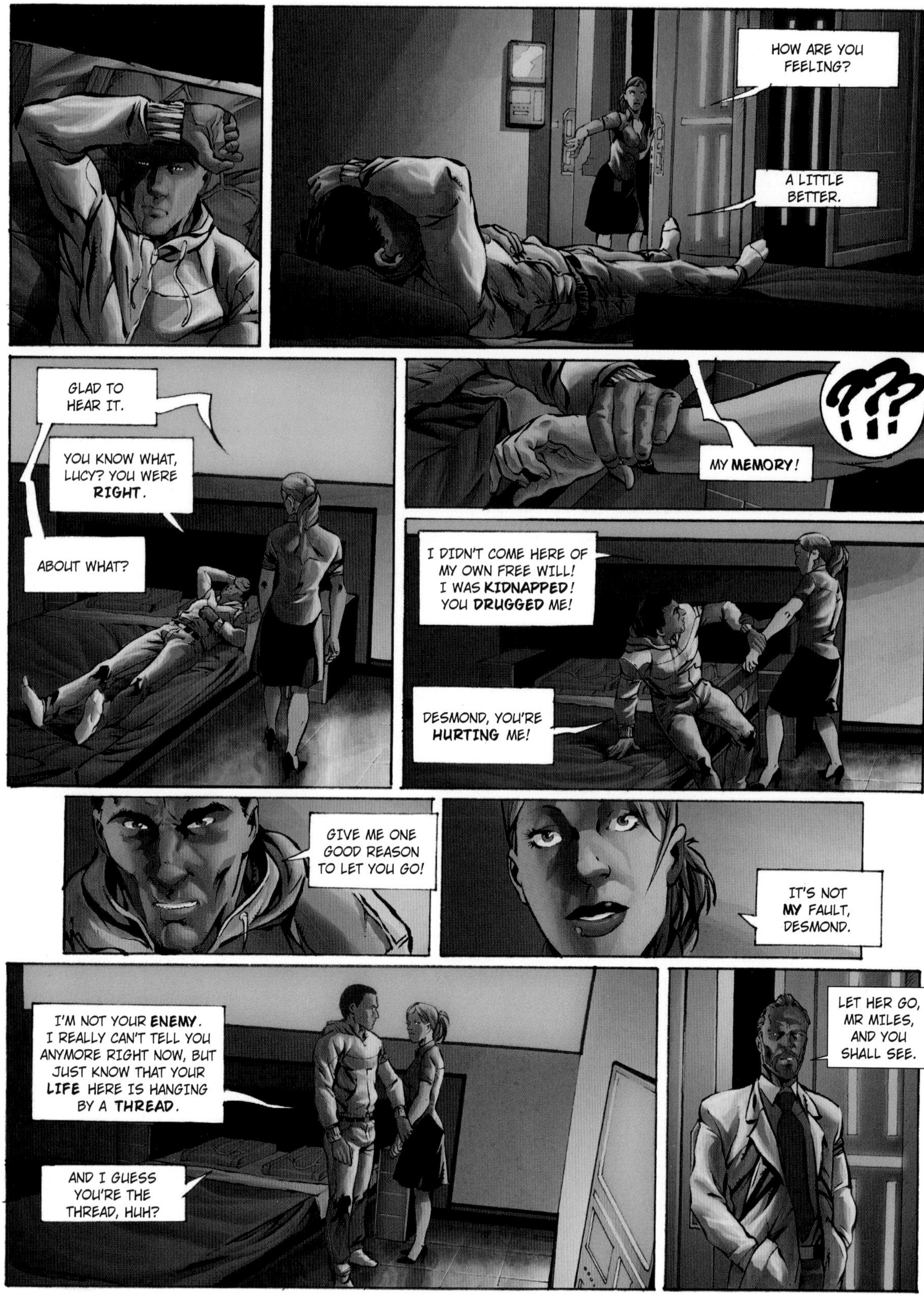
HOW ARE YOU FEELING?
A LITTLE BETTER.
GLAD TO HEAR IT.
YOU KNOW WHAT, LUCY? YOU WERE RIGHT.
ABOUT WHAT?
MY MEMORY!
???
I DIDN'T COME HERE OF MY OWN FREE WILL! I WAS KIDNAPPED! YOU DRUGGED ME!
DESMOND, YOU'RE HURTING ME!
GIVE ME ONE GOOD REASON TO LET YOU GO!
IT'S NOT MY FAULT, DESMOND.
I'M NOT YOUR ENEMY. I REALLY CAN'T TELL YOU ANYMORE RIGHT NOW, BUT JUST KNOW THAT YOUR LIFE HERE IS HANGING BY A THREAD.
AND I GUESS YOU'RE THE THREAD, HUH?
LET HER GO, MR MILES, AND YOU SHALL SEE.

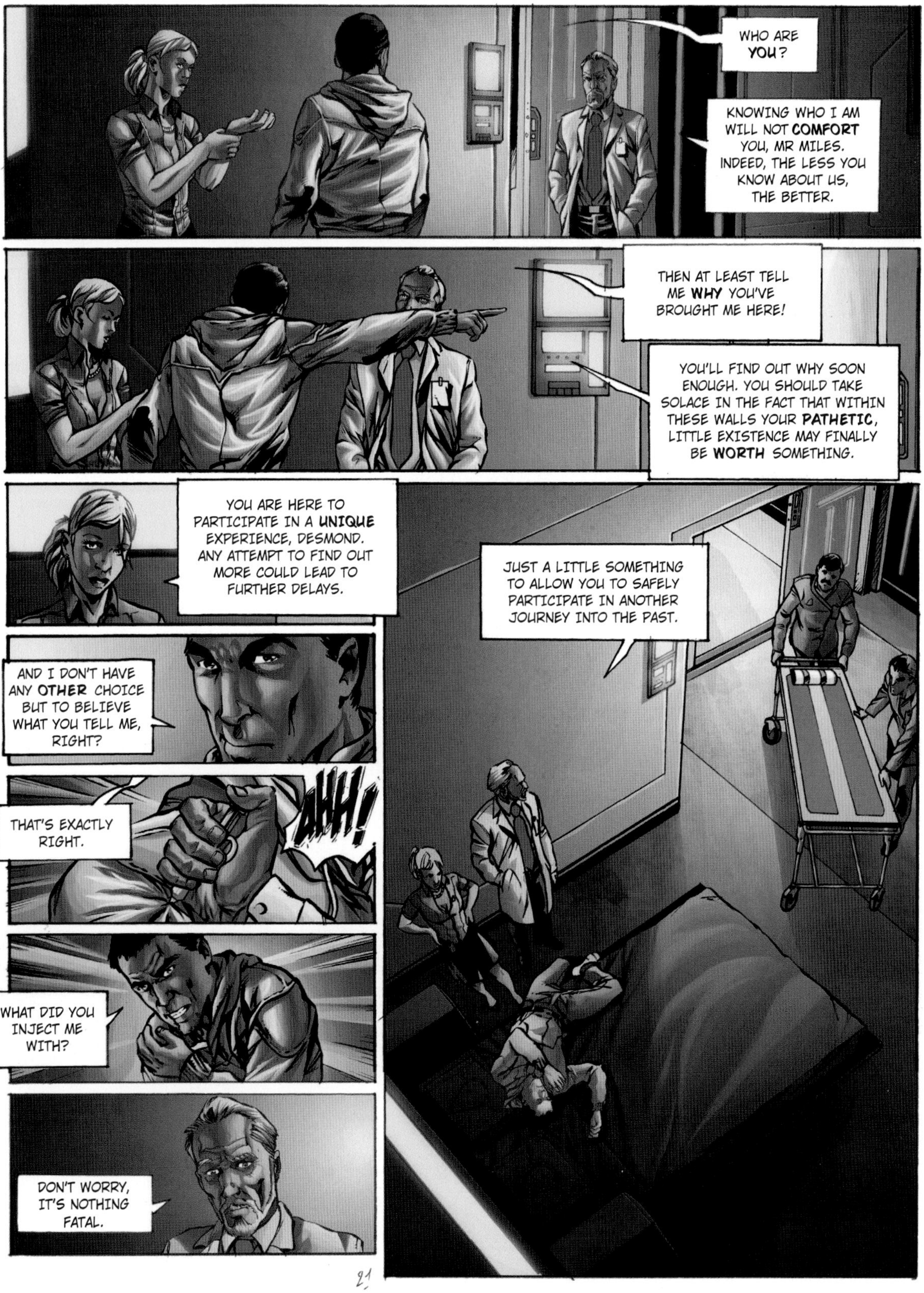
WHO ARE YOU?
KNOWING WHO I AM WILL NOT COMFORT YOU, MR MILES. INDEED, THE LESS YOU KNOW ABOUT US, THE BETTER.
THEN AT LEAST TELL ME WHY YOU'VE BROUGHT ME HERE!
YOU'LL FIND OUT WHY SOON ENOUGH. YOU SHOULD TAKE SOLACE IN THE FACT THAT WITHIN THESE WALLS YOUR PATHETIC, LITTLE EXISTENCE MAY FINALLY BE WORTH SOMETHING.
YOU ARE HERE TO PARTICIPATE IN A UNIQUE EXPERIENCE, DESMOND. ANY ATTEMPT TO FIND OUT MORE COULD LEAD TO FURTHER DELAYS.
AND I DON'T HAVE ANY OTHER CHOICE BUT TO BELIEVE WHAT YOU TELL ME, RIGHT?
THAT'S EXACTLY RIGHT.
AHH!
WHAT DID YOU INJECT ME WITH?
DON'T WORRY, IT'S NOTHING FATAL.
JUST A LITTLE SOMETHING TO ALLOW YOU TO SAFELY PARTICIPATE IN ANOTHER JOURNEY INTO THE PAST.
21

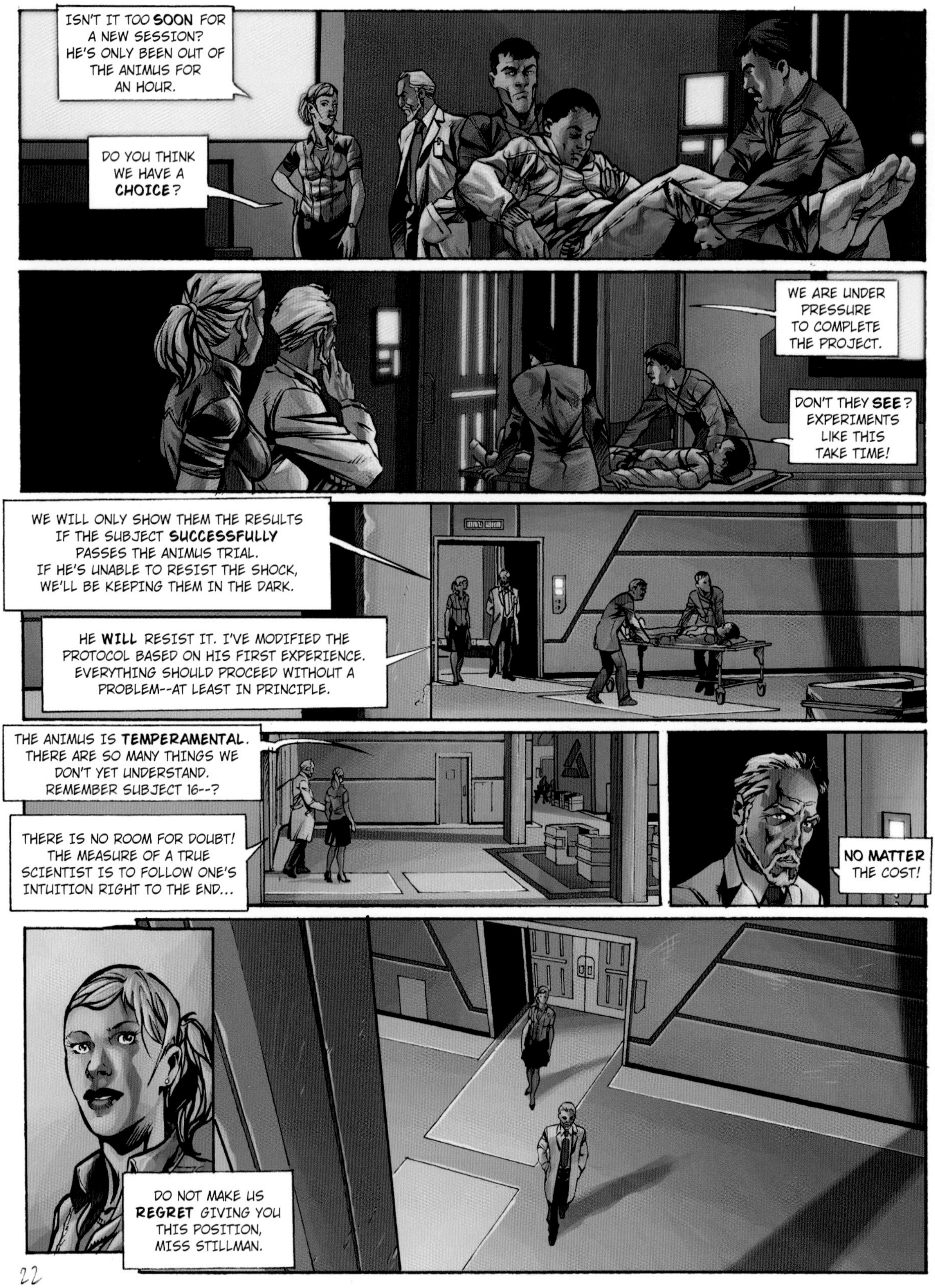
ISN'T IT TOO SOON FOR A NEW SESSION? HE'S ONLY BEEN OUT OF THE ANIMUS FOR AN HOUR.
DO YOU THINK WE HAVE A CHOICE?
WE ARE UNDER PRESSURE TO COMPLETE THE PROJECT.
DON'T THEY SEE? EXPERIMENTS LIKE THIS TAKE TIME!
WE WILL ONLY SHOW THEM THE RESULTS IF THE SUBJECT SUCCESSFULLY PASSES THE ANIMUS TRIAL. IF HE'S UNABLE TO RESIST THE SHOCK, WE'LL BE KEEPING THEM IN THE DARK.
HE WILL RESIST IT. I'VE MODIFIED THE PROTOCOL BASED ON HIS FIRST EXPERIENCE. EVERYTHING SHOULD PROCEED WITHOUT A PROBLEM--AT LEAST IN PRINCIPLE.
THE ANIMUS IS TEMPERAMENTAL. THERE ARE SO MANY THINGS WE DON'T YET UNDERSTAND. REMEMBER SUBJECT 16--?
THERE IS NO ROOM FOR DOUBT! THE MEASURE OF A TRUE SCIENTIST IS TO FOLLOW ONE'S INTUITION RIGHT TO THE END...
NO MATTER THE COST!
DO NOT MAKE US REGRET GIVING YOU THIS POSITION, MISS STILLMAN.
22

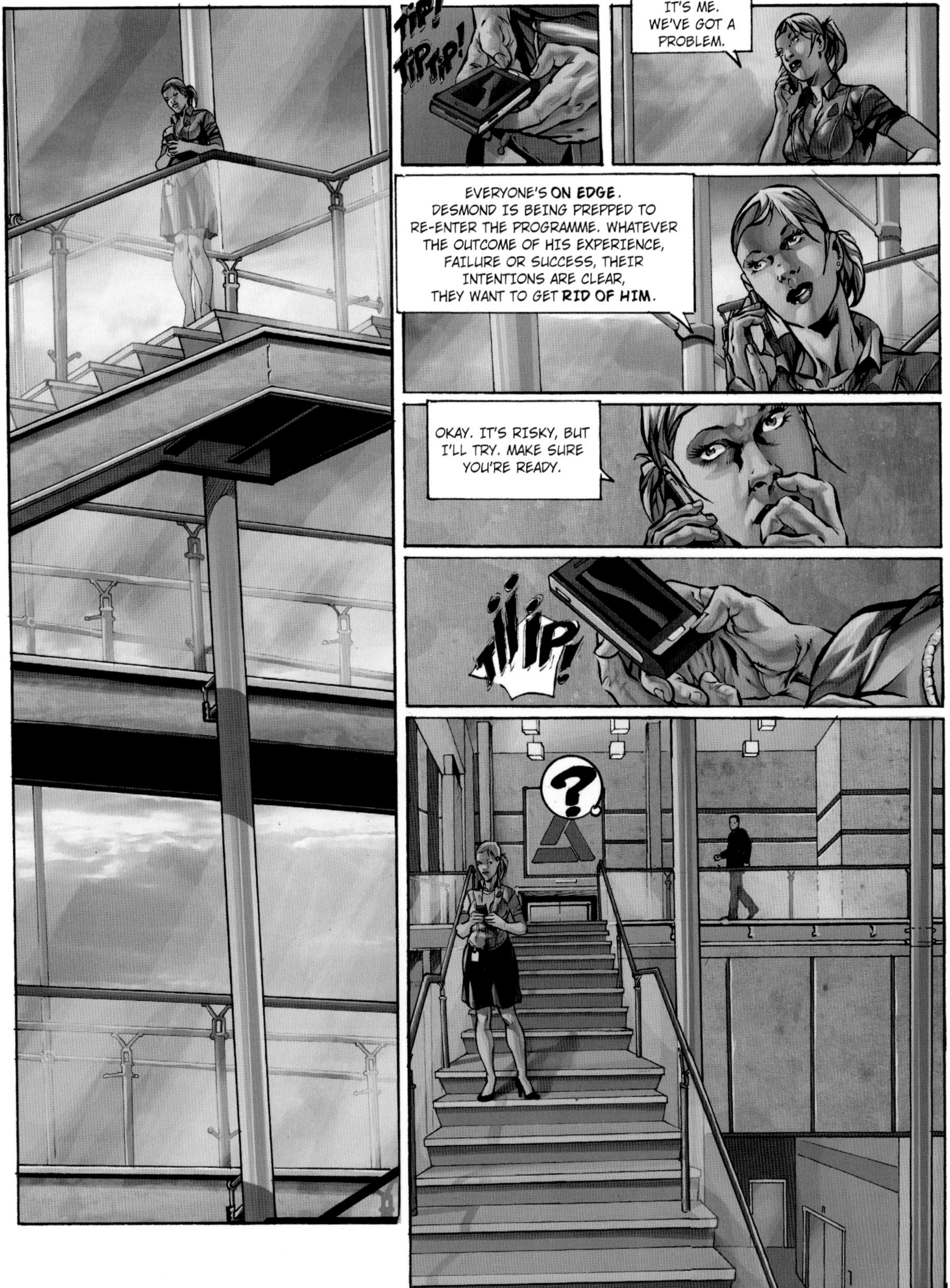
TIP!
TIP TIP!
IT'S ME.
WE'VE GOT A
PROBLEM.
EVERYONE'S ON EDGE.
DESMOND IS BEING PREPPED TO
RE-ENTER THE PROGRAMME. WHATEVER
THE OUTCOME OF HIS EXPERIENCE,
FAILURE OR SUCCESS, THEIR
INTENTIONS ARE CLEAR,
THEY WANT TO GET RID OF HIM.
OKAY. IT'S RISKY, BUT
I'LL TRY. MAKE SURE
YOU'RE READY.
TIIIP!
?
23

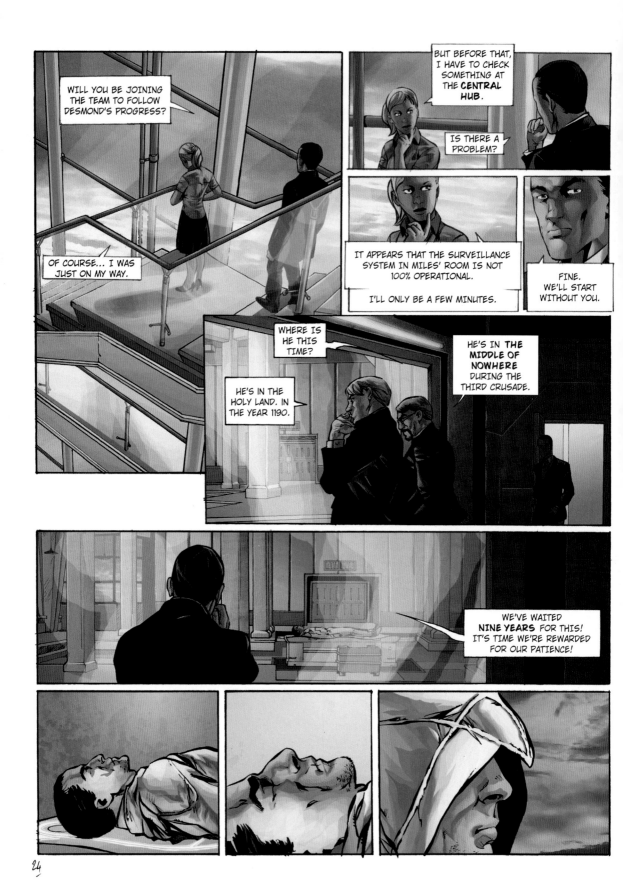

WILL YOU BE JOINING THE TEAM TO FOLLOW DESMOND'S PROGRESS?

OF COURSE... I WAS JUST ON MY WAY.

BUT BEFORE THAT, I HAVE TO CHECK SOMETHING AT THE **CENTRAL HUB**.

IS THERE A PROBLEM?

IT APPEARS THAT THE SURVEILLANCE SYSTEM IN MILES' ROOM IS NOT 100% OPERATIONAL.

I'LL ONLY BE A FEW MINUTES.

FINE. WE'LL START WITHOUT YOU.

WHERE IS HE THIS TIME?

HE'S IN THE HOLY LAND. IN THE YEAR 1190.

HE'S IN **THE MIDDLE OF NOWHERE** DURING THE THIRD CRUSADE.

WE'VE WAITED **NINE YEARS** FOR THIS! IT'S TIME WE'RE REWARDED FOR OUR PATIENCE!

24

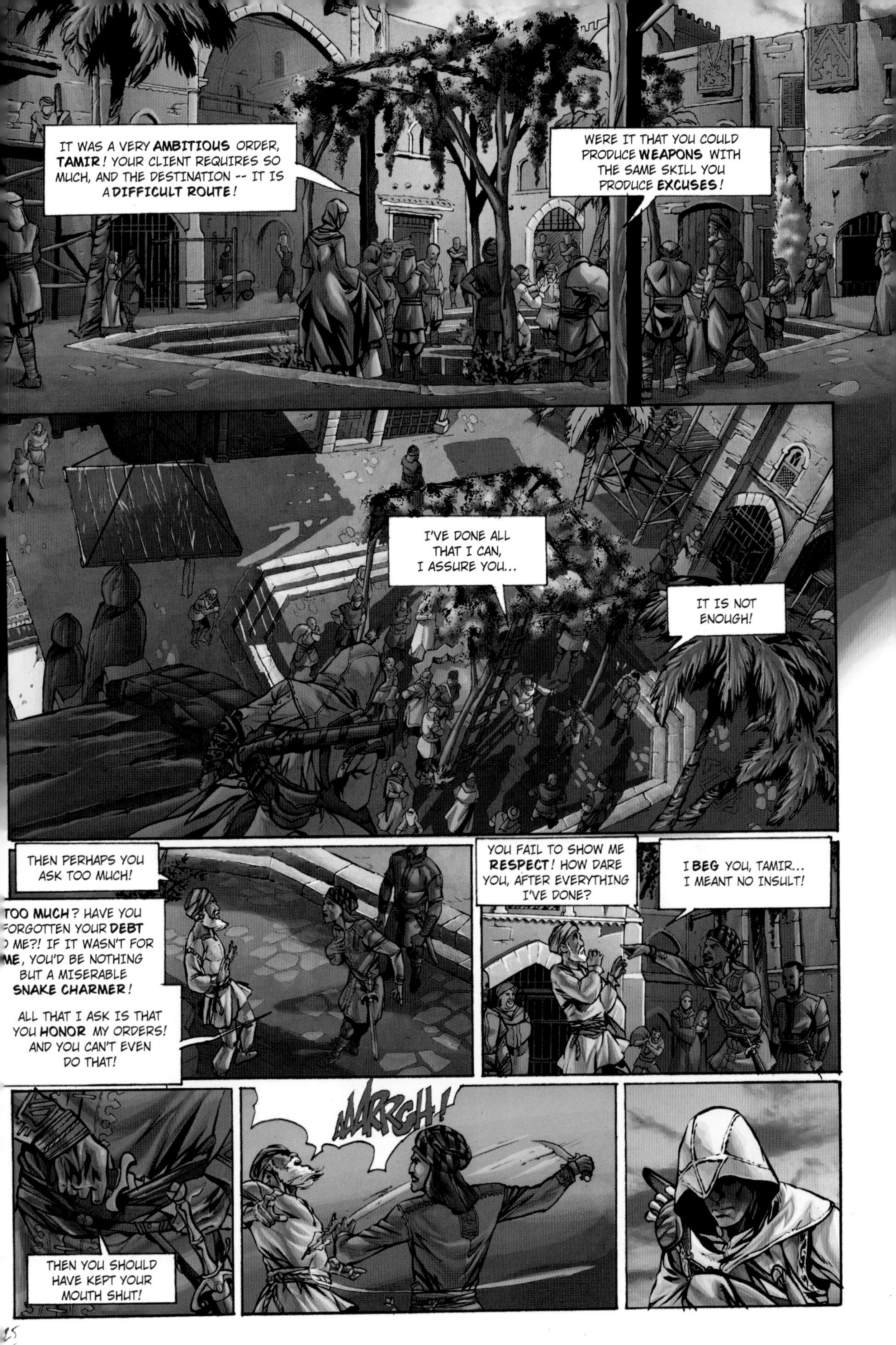
IT WAS A VERY AMBITIOUS ORDER, TAMIR! YOUR CLIENT REQUIRES SO MUCH, AND THE DESTINATION -- IT IS A DIFFICULT ROUTE!
WERE IT THAT YOU COULD PRODUCE WEAPONS WITH THE SAME SKILL YOU PRODUCE EXCUSES!
I'VE DONE ALL THAT I CAN, I ASSURE YOU...
IT IS NOT ENOUGH!
THEN PERHAPS YOU ASK TOO MUCH!
TOO MUCH? HAVE YOU FORGOTTEN YOUR DEBT TO ME?! IF IT WASN'T FOR ME, YOU'D BE NOTHING BUT A MISERABLE SNAKE CHARMER!
ALL THAT I ASK IS THAT YOU HONOR MY ORDERS! AND YOU CAN'T EVEN DO THAT!
YOU FAIL TO SHOW ME RESPECT! HOW DARE YOU, AFTER EVERYTHING I'VE DONE?
I BEG YOU, TAMIR... I MEANT NO INSULT!
THEN YOU SHOULD HAVE KEPT YOUR MOUTH SHUT!
AAARRGH!

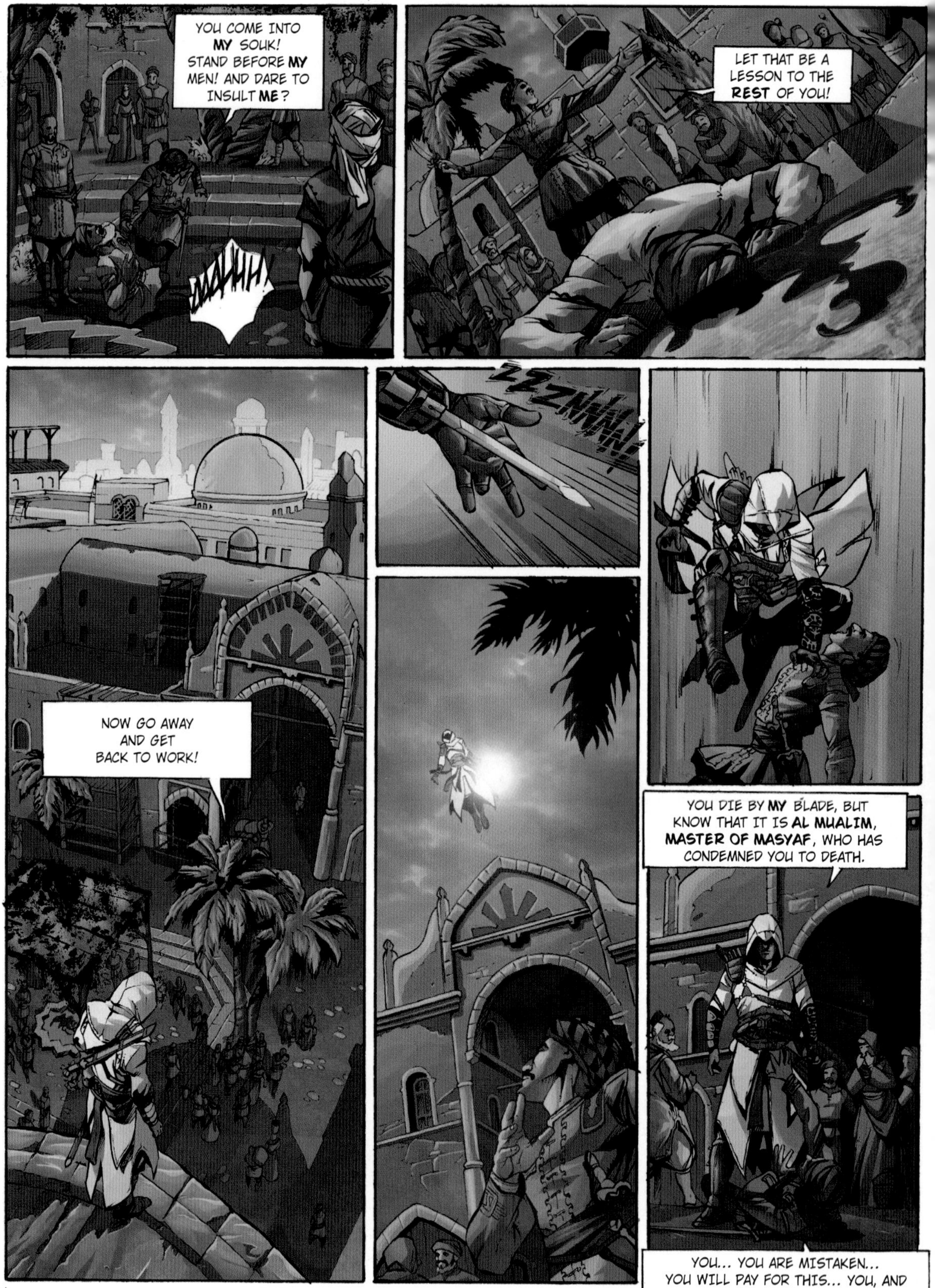
YOU COME INTO MY SOUK! STAND BEFORE MY MEN! AND DARE TO INSULT ME?
LET THAT BE A LESSON TO THE REST OF YOU!
NOW GO AWAY AND GET BACK TO WORK!
ZZZNNNN!
YOU DIE BY MY BLADE, BUT KNOW THAT IT IS AL MUALIM, MASTER OF MASYAF, WHO HAS CONDEMNED YOU TO DEATH.
YOU... YOU ARE MISTAKEN... YOU WILL PAY FOR THIS... YOU, AND ALL YOUR KIND!

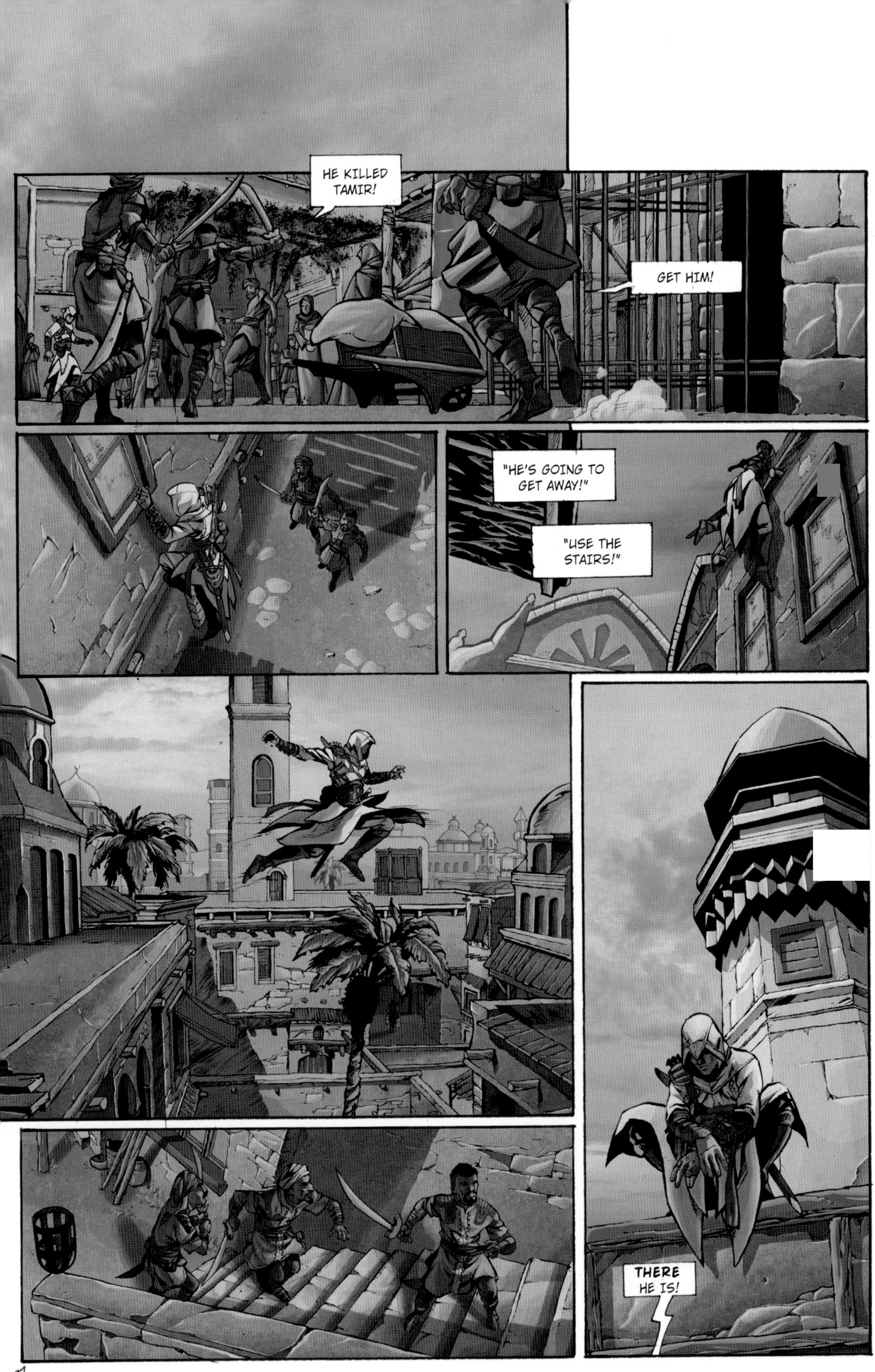
HE KILLED TAMIR!
GET HIM!
"HE'S GOING TO GET AWAY!"
"USE THE STAIRS!"
THERE HE IS!

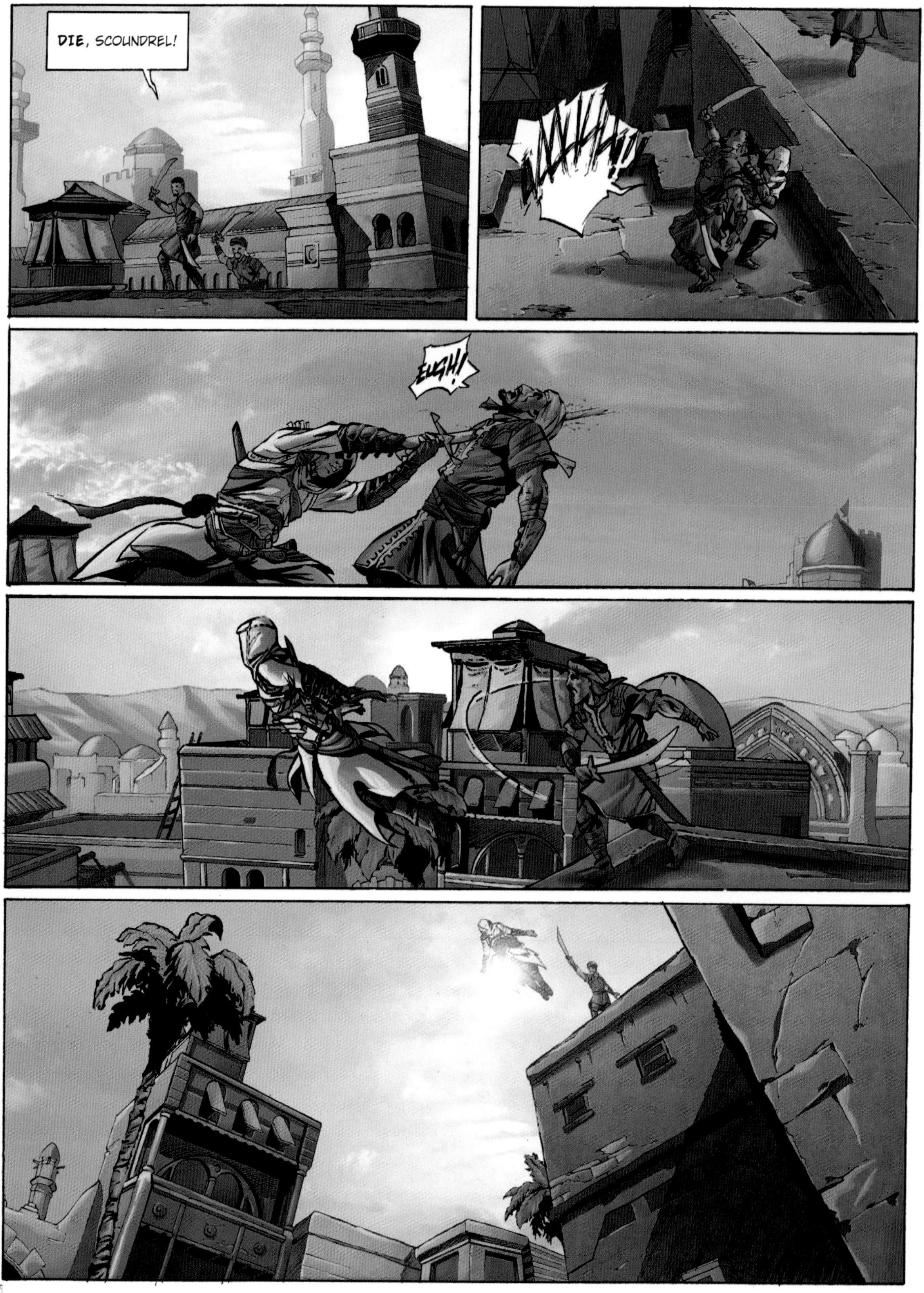
DIE, SCOUNDREL!
EUGH!

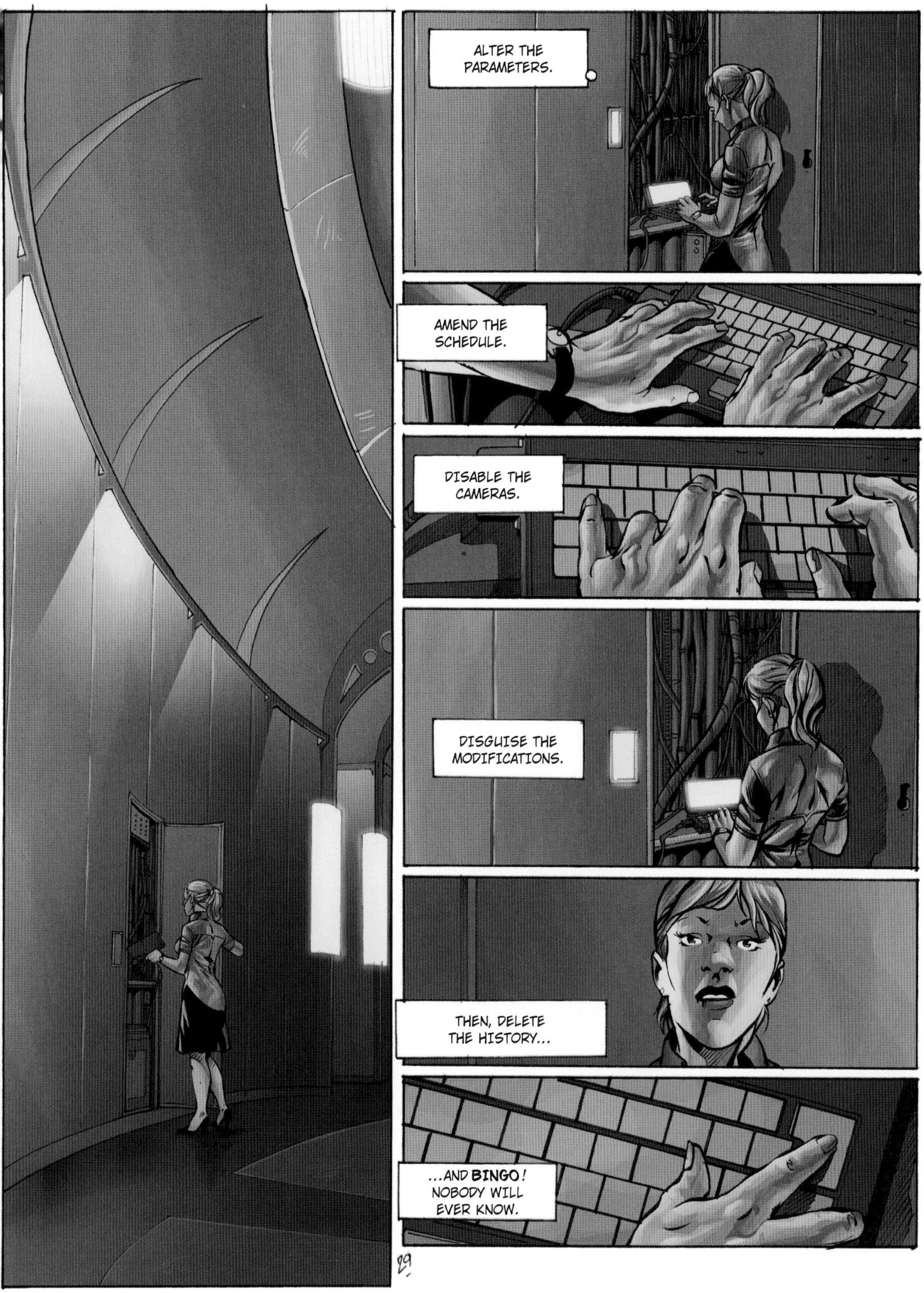
ALTER THE PARAMETERS.
AMEND THE SCHEDULE.
DISABLE THE CAMERAS.
DISGUISE THE MODIFICATIONS.
THEN, DELETE THE HISTORY...
...AND BINGO! NOBODY WILL EVER KNOW.
29

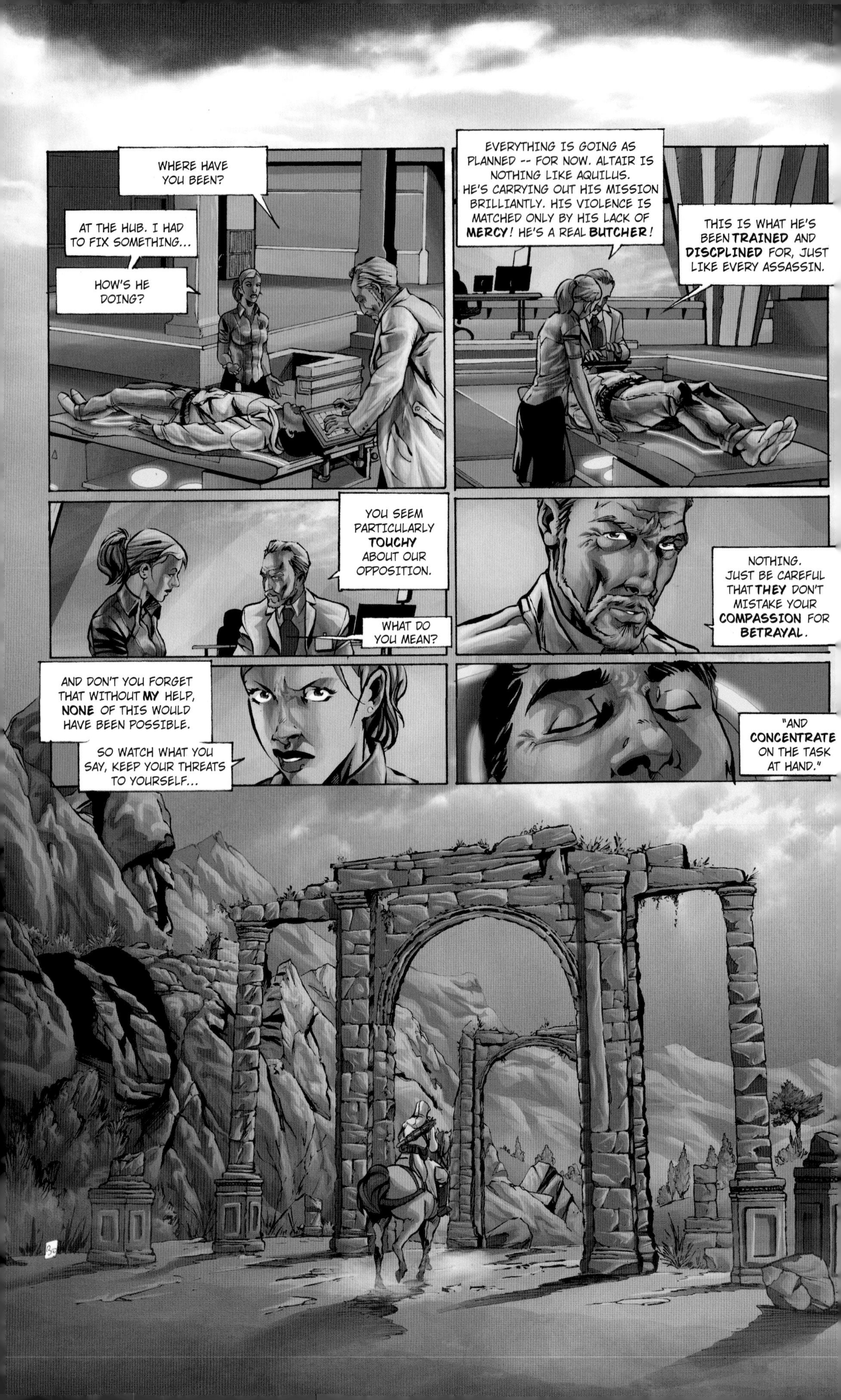
WHERE HAVE YOU BEEN?
AT THE HUB. I HAD TO FIX SOMETHING...
HOW'S HE DOING?
EVERYTHING IS GOING AS PLANNED -- FOR NOW. ALTAIR IS NOTHING LIKE AQUILUS. HE'S CARRYING OUT HIS MISSION BRILLIANTLY. HIS VIOLENCE IS MATCHED ONLY BY HIS LACK OF MERCY! HE'S A REAL BUTCHER!
THIS IS WHAT HE'S BEEN TRAINED AND DISCPLINED FOR, JUST LIKE EVERY ASSASSIN.
YOU SEEM PARTICULARLY TOUCHY ABOUT OUR OPPOSITION.
WHAT DO YOU MEAN?
NOTHING. JUST BE CAREFUL THAT THEY DON'T MISTAKE YOUR COMPASSION FOR BETRAYAL.
AND DON'T YOU FORGET THAT WITHOUT MY HELP, NONE OF THIS WOULD HAVE BEEN POSSIBLE.
SO WATCH WHAT YOU SAY, KEEP YOUR THREATS TO YOURSELF...
"AND CONCENTRATE ON THE TASK AT HAND."

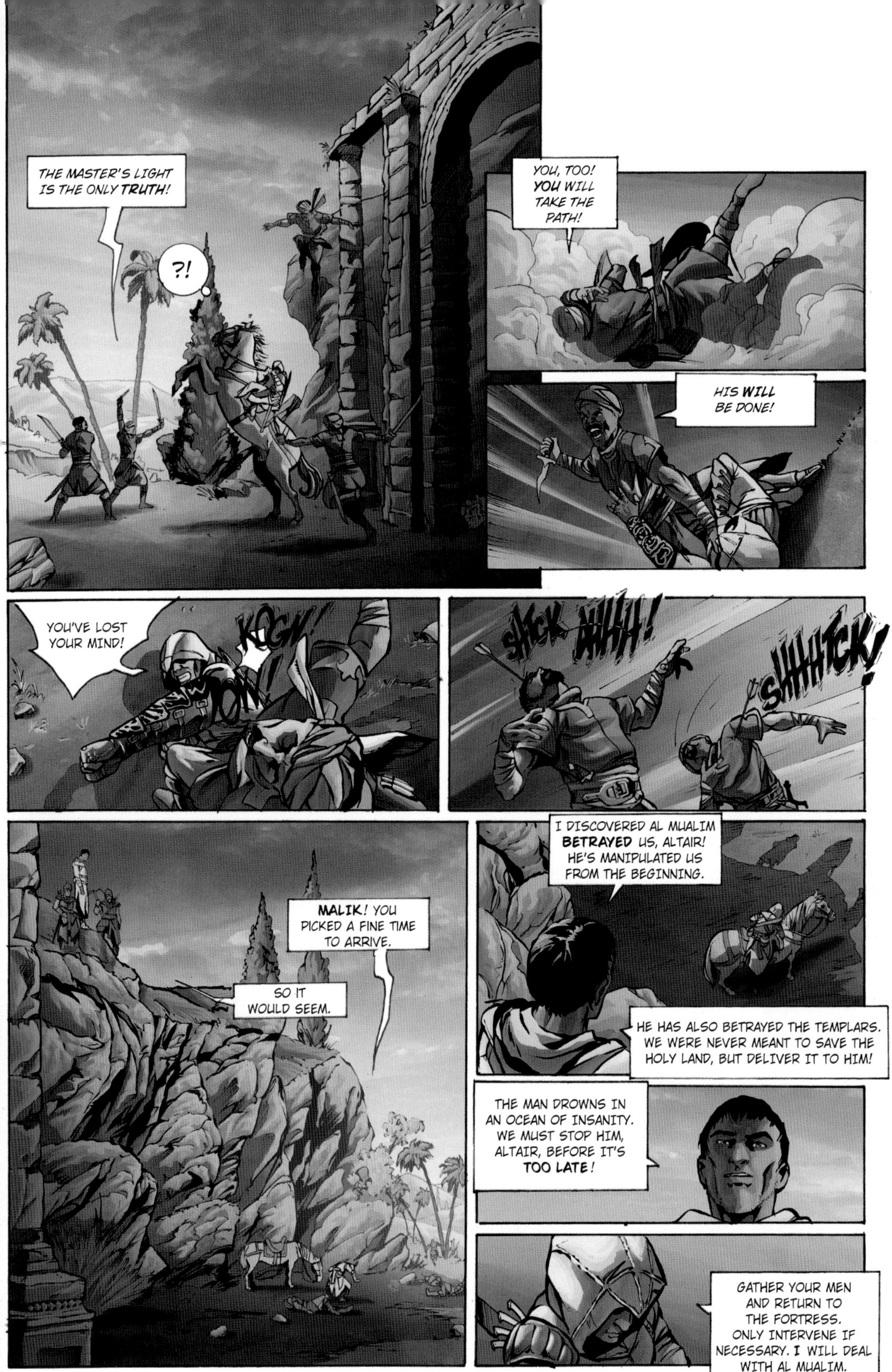
THE MASTER'S LIGHT IS THE ONLY TRUTH!
?!
YOU, TOO! YOU WILL TAKE THE PATH!
HIS WILL BE DONE!
YOU'VE LOST YOUR MIND!
KOGH!
SHICK
AHHH!
SHHHTCK!
MALIK! YOU PICKED A FINE TIME TO ARRIVE.
SO IT WOULD SEEM.
I DISCOVERED AL MUALIM BETRAYED US, ALTAIR! HE'S MANIPULATED US FROM THE BEGINNING.
HE HAS ALSO BETRAYED THE TEMPLARS. WE WERE NEVER MEANT TO SAVE THE HOLY LAND, BUT DELIVER IT TO HIM!
THE MAN DROWNS IN AN OCEAN OF INSANITY. WE MUST STOP HIM, ALTAIR, BEFORE IT'S TOO LATE!
GATHER YOUR MEN AND RETURN TO THE FORTRESS. ONLY INTERVENE IF NECESSARY. I WILL DEAL WITH AL MUALIM.

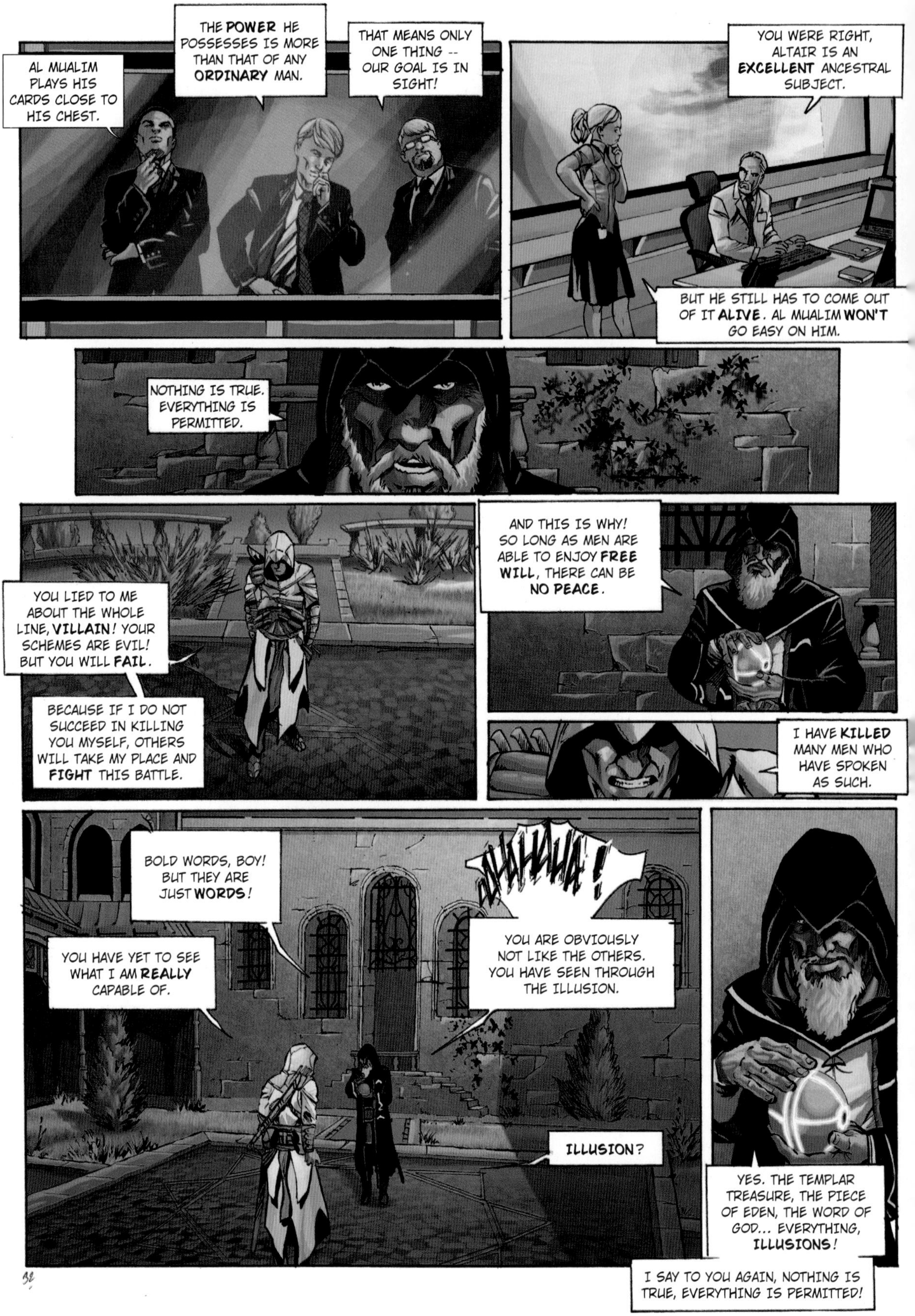
AL MUALIM PLAYS HIS CARDS CLOSE TO HIS CHEST.
THE **POWER** HE POSSESSES IS MORE THAN THAT OF ANY **ORDINARY** MAN.
THAT MEANS ONLY ONE THING -- OUR GOAL IS IN SIGHT!
YOU WERE RIGHT, ALTAIR IS AN **EXCELLENT** ANCESTRAL SUBJECT.
BUT HE STILL HAS TO COME OUT OF IT **ALIVE**. AL MUALIM **WON'T** GO EASY ON HIM.
NOTHING IS TRUE. EVERYTHING IS PERMITTED.
YOU LIED TO ME ABOUT THE WHOLE LINE, **VILLAIN**! YOUR SCHEMES ARE EVIL! BUT YOU WILL **FAIL**.
BECAUSE IF I DO NOT SUCCEED IN KILLING YOU MYSELF, OTHERS WILL TAKE MY PLACE AND **FIGHT** THIS BATTLE.
AND THIS IS WHY! SO LONG AS MEN ARE ABLE TO ENJOY **FREE WILL**, THERE CAN BE **NO PEACE**.
I HAVE **KILLED** MANY MEN WHO HAVE SPOKEN AS SUCH.
BOLD WORDS, BOY! BUT THEY ARE JUST **WORDS**!
YOU HAVE YET TO SEE WHAT I AM **REALLY** CAPABLE OF.
YOU ARE OBVIOUSLY NOT LIKE THE OTHERS. YOU HAVE SEEN THROUGH THE ILLUSION.
ILLUSION?
YES. THE TEMPLAR TREASURE, THE PIECE OF EDEN, THE WORD OF GOD... EVERYTHING, **ILLUSIONS**!
I SAY TO YOU AGAIN, NOTHING IS TRUE, EVERYTHING IS PERMITTED!

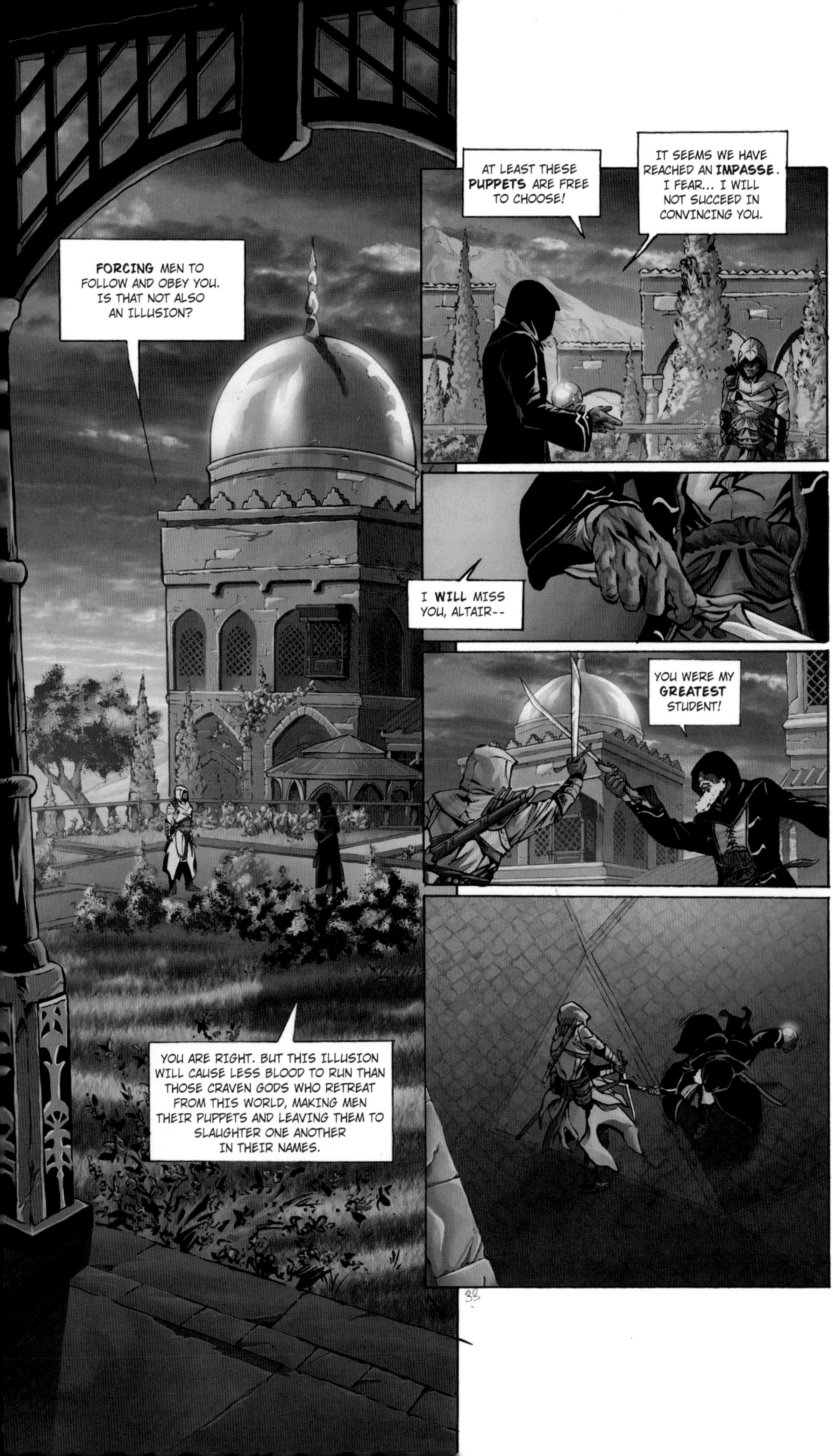
FORCING MEN TO FOLLOW AND OBEY YOU. IS THAT NOT ALSO AN ILLUSION?
YOU ARE RIGHT. BUT THIS ILLUSION WILL CAUSE LESS BLOOD TO RUN THAN THOSE CRAVEN GODS WHO RETREAT FROM THIS WORLD, MAKING MEN THEIR PUPPETS AND LEAVING THEM TO SLAUGHTER ONE ANOTHER IN THEIR NAMES.
AT LEAST THESE PUPPETS ARE FREE TO CHOOSE!
IT SEEMS WE HAVE REACHED AN IMPASSE. I FEAR... I WILL NOT SUCCEED IN CONVINCING YOU.
I WILL MISS YOU, ALTAIR--
YOU WERE MY GREATEST STUDENT!

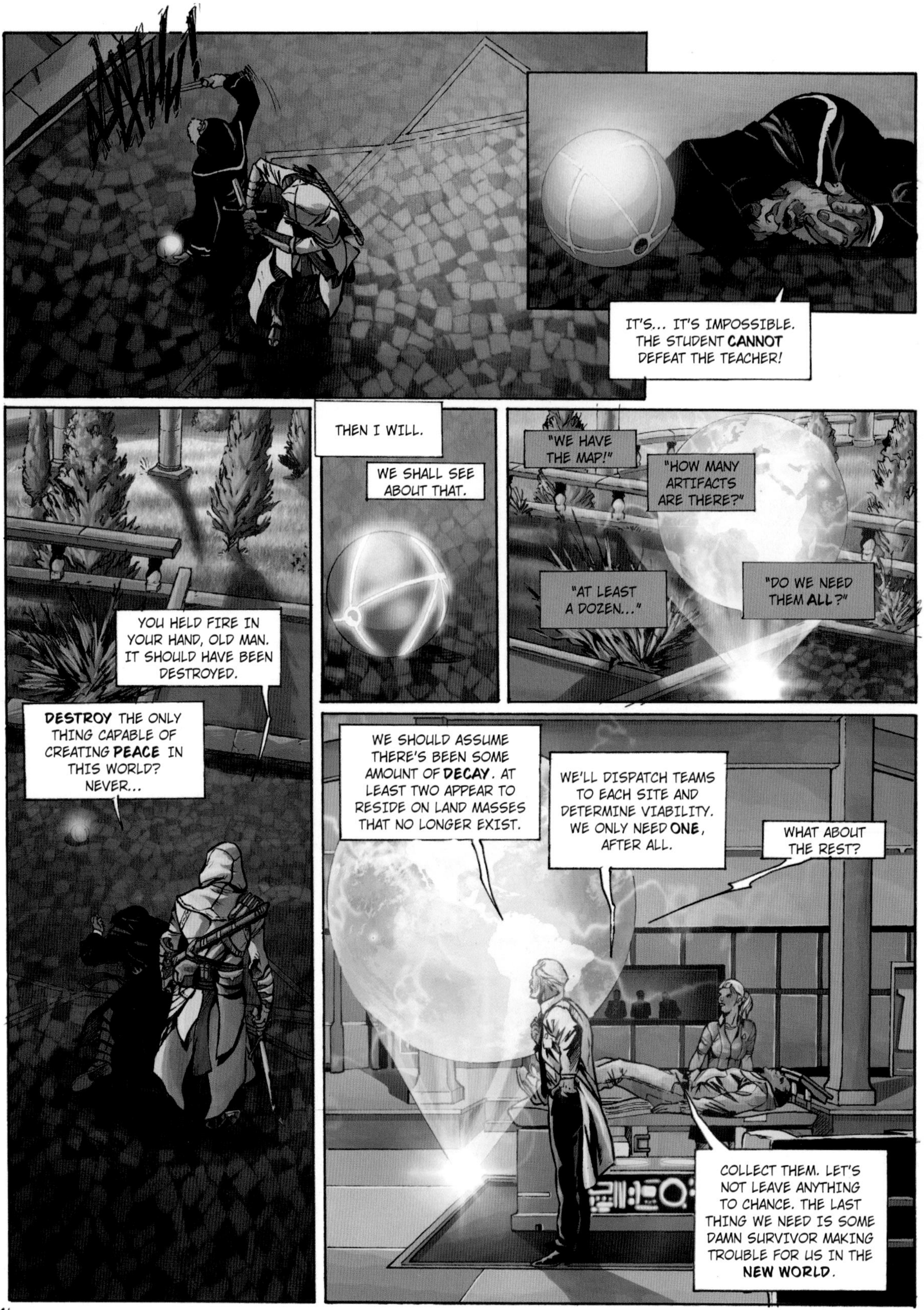
AAAHHH!
IT'S... IT'S IMPOSSIBLE. THE STUDENT **CANNOT** DEFEAT THE TEACHER!
THEN I WILL.
WE SHALL SEE ABOUT THAT.
"WE HAVE THE MAP!"
"HOW MANY ARTIFACTS ARE THERE?"
"AT LEAST A DOZEN..."
"DO WE NEED THEM **ALL**?"
YOU HELD FIRE IN YOUR HAND, OLD MAN. IT SHOULD HAVE BEEN DESTROYED.
DESTROY THE ONLY THING CAPABLE OF CREATING **PEACE** IN THIS WORLD? NEVER...
WE SHOULD ASSUME THERE'S BEEN SOME AMOUNT OF **DECAY**. AT LEAST TWO APPEAR TO RESIDE ON LAND MASSES THAT NO LONGER EXIST.
WE'LL DISPATCH TEAMS TO EACH SITE AND DETERMINE VIABILITY. WE ONLY NEED **ONE**, AFTER ALL.
WHAT ABOUT THE REST?
COLLECT THEM. LET'S NOT LEAVE ANYTHING TO CHANCE. THE LAST THING WE NEED IS SOME DAMN SURVIVOR MAKING TROUBLE FOR US IN THE **NEW WORLD**.

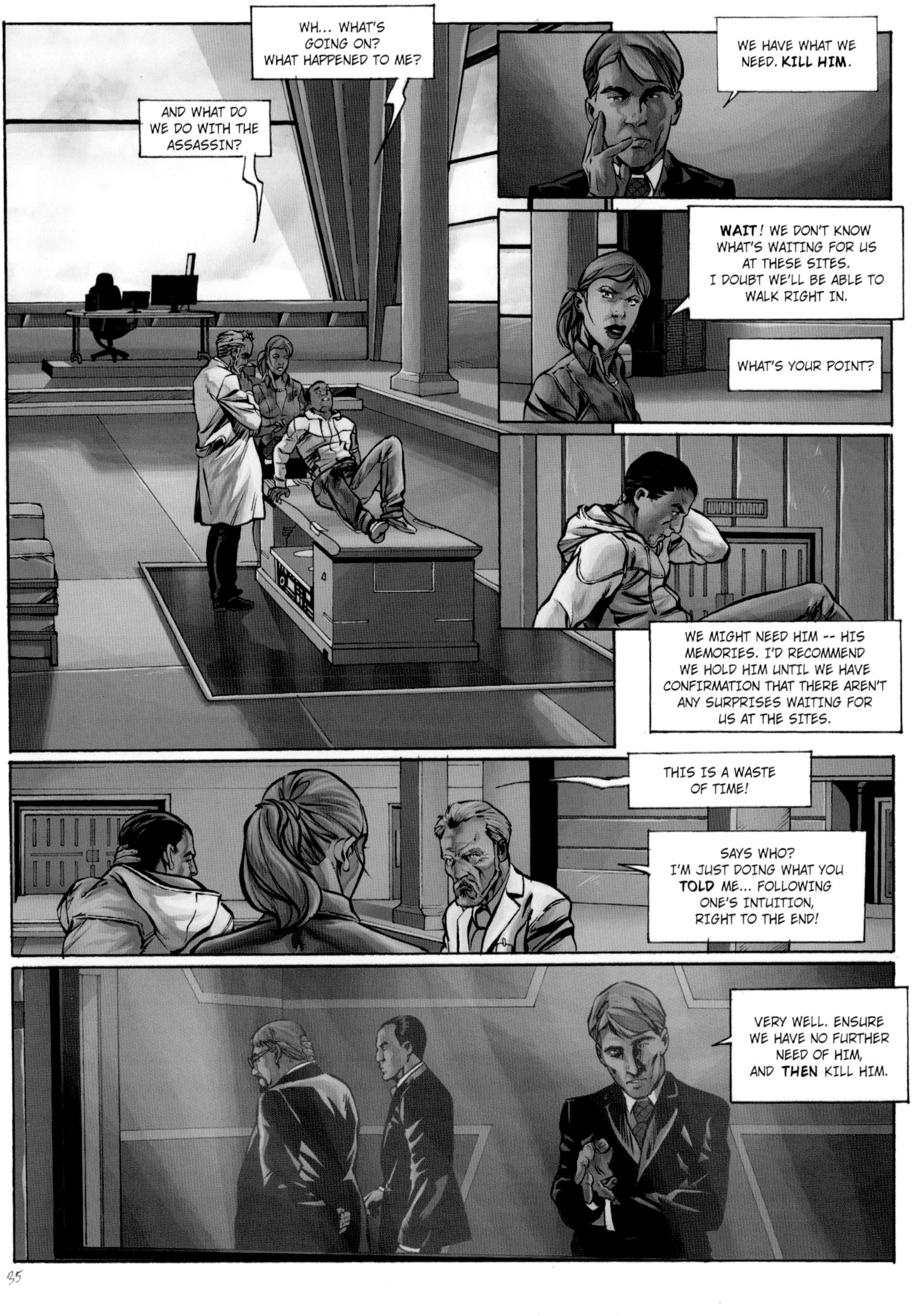
AND WHAT DO WE DO WITH THE ASSASSIN?
WH... WHAT'S GOING ON? WHAT HAPPENED TO ME?
WE HAVE WHAT WE NEED. KILL HIM.
WAIT! WE DON'T KNOW WHAT'S WAITING FOR US AT THESE SITES. I DOUBT WE'LL BE ABLE TO WALK RIGHT IN.
WHAT'S YOUR POINT?
WE MIGHT NEED HIM -- HIS MEMORIES. I'D RECOMMEND WE HOLD HIM UNTIL WE HAVE CONFIRMATION THAT THERE AREN'T ANY SURPRISES WAITING FOR US AT THE SITES.
THIS IS A WASTE OF TIME!
SAYS WHO? I'M JUST DOING WHAT YOU TOLD ME... FOLLOWING ONE'S INTUITION, RIGHT TO THE END!
VERY WELL. ENSURE WE HAVE NO FURTHER NEED OF HIM, AND THEN KILL HIM.
35

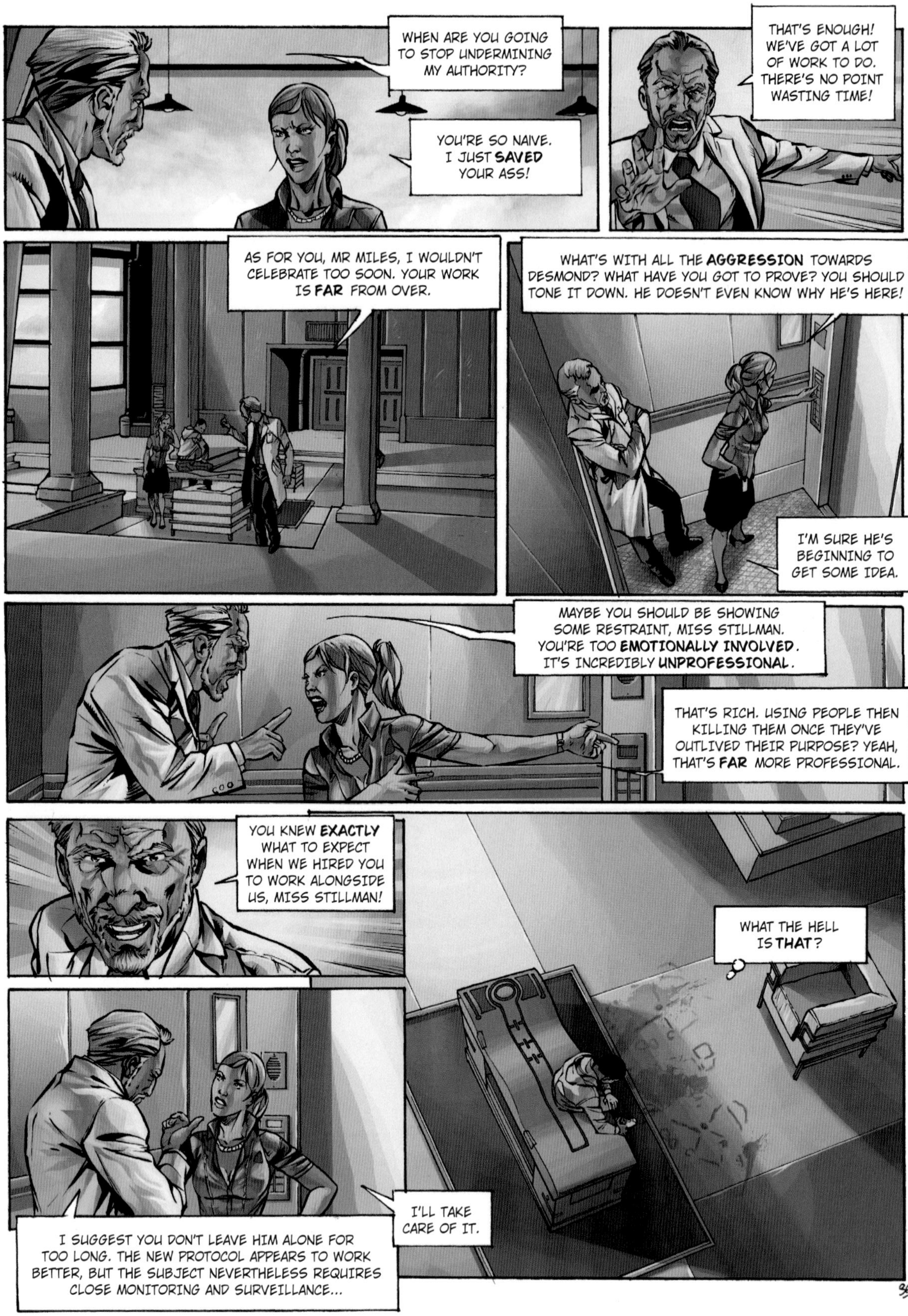

WHEN ARE YOU GOING TO STOP UNDERMINING MY AUTHORITY?
YOU'RE SO NAIVE. I JUST **SAVED** YOUR ASS!
THAT'S ENOUGH! WE'VE GOT A LOT OF WORK TO DO. THERE'S NO POINT WASTING TIME!
AS FOR YOU, MR MILES, I WOULDN'T CELEBRATE TOO SOON. YOUR WORK IS **FAR** FROM OVER.
WHAT'S WITH ALL THE **AGGRESSION** TOWARDS DESMOND? WHAT HAVE YOU GOT TO PROVE? YOU SHOULD TONE IT DOWN. HE DOESN'T EVEN KNOW WHY HE'S HERE!
I'M SURE HE'S BEGINNING TO GET SOME IDEA.
MAYBE YOU SHOULD BE SHOWING SOME RESTRAINT, MISS STILLMAN. YOU'RE TOO **EMOTIONALLY INVOLVED**. IT'S INCREDIBLY **UNPROFESSIONAL**.
THAT'S RICH. USING PEOPLE THEN KILLING THEM ONCE THEY'VE OUTLIVED THEIR PURPOSE? YEAH, THAT'S **FAR** MORE PROFESSIONAL.
YOU KNEW **EXACTLY** WHAT TO EXPECT WHEN WE HIRED YOU TO WORK ALONGSIDE US, MISS STILLMAN!
I SUGGEST YOU DON'T LEAVE HIM ALONE FOR TOO LONG. THE NEW PROTOCOL APPEARS TO WORK BETTER, BUT THE SUBJECT NEVERTHELESS REQUIRES CLOSE MONITORING AND SURVEILLANCE...
I'LL TAKE CARE OF IT.
WHAT THE HELL IS **THAT**?

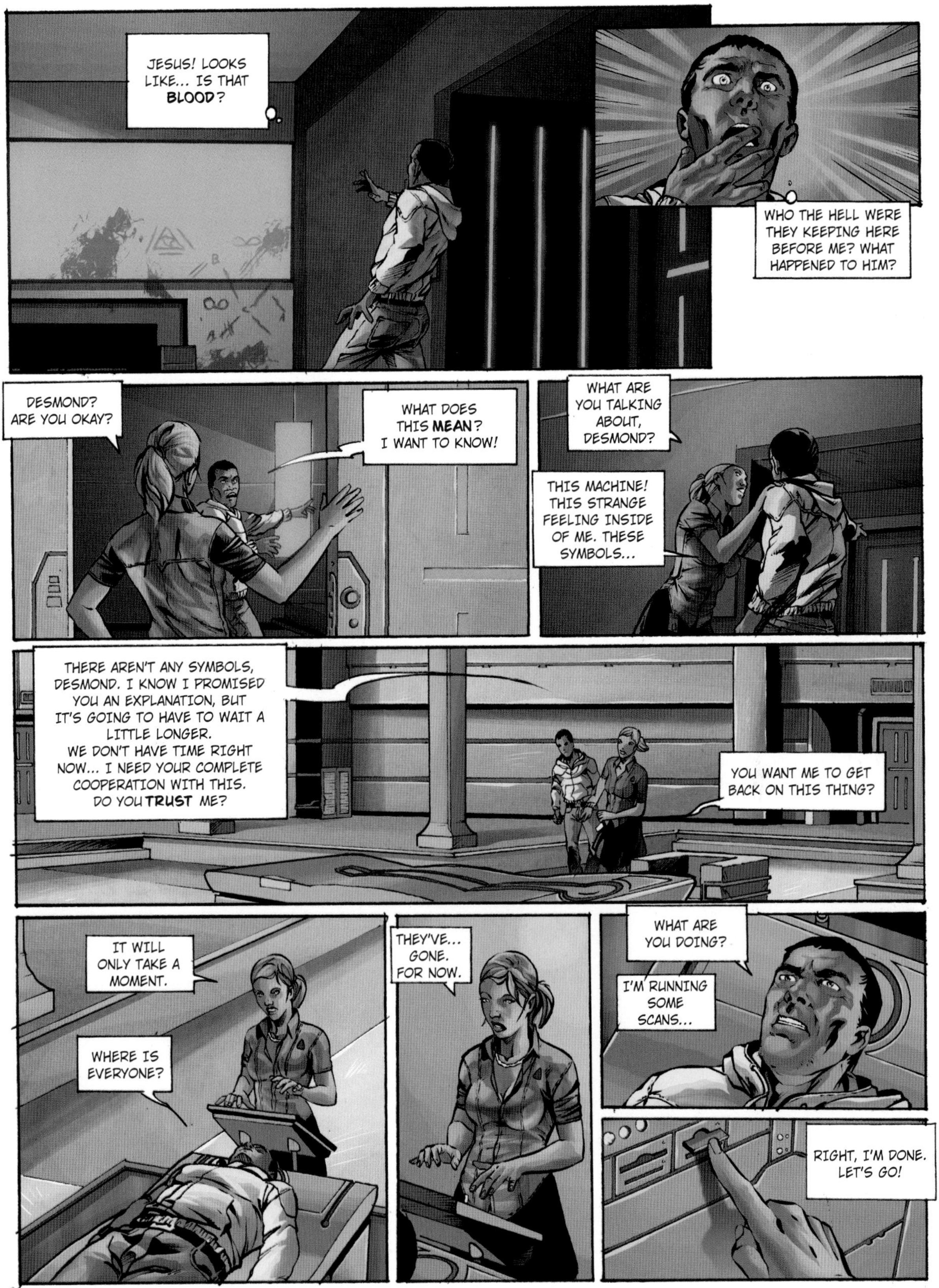

JESUS! LOOKS LIKE... IS THAT **BLOOD**?
WHO THE HELL WERE THEY KEEPING HERE BEFORE ME? WHAT HAPPENED TO HIM?
DESMOND? ARE YOU OKAY?
WHAT DOES THIS **MEAN**? I WANT TO KNOW!
WHAT ARE YOU TALKING ABOUT, DESMOND?
THIS MACHINE! THIS STRANGE FEELING INSIDE OF ME. THESE SYMBOLS...
THERE AREN'T ANY SYMBOLS, DESMOND. I KNOW I PROMISED YOU AN EXPLANATION, BUT IT'S GOING TO HAVE TO WAIT A LITTLE LONGER. WE DON'T HAVE TIME RIGHT NOW... I NEED YOUR COMPLETE COOPERATION WITH THIS. DO YOU **TRUST** ME?
YOU WANT ME TO GET BACK ON THIS THING?
IT WILL ONLY TAKE A MOMENT.
WHERE IS EVERYONE?
THEY'VE... GONE. FOR NOW.
WHAT ARE YOU DOING?
I'M RUNNING SOME SCANS...
RIGHT, I'M DONE. LET'S GO!

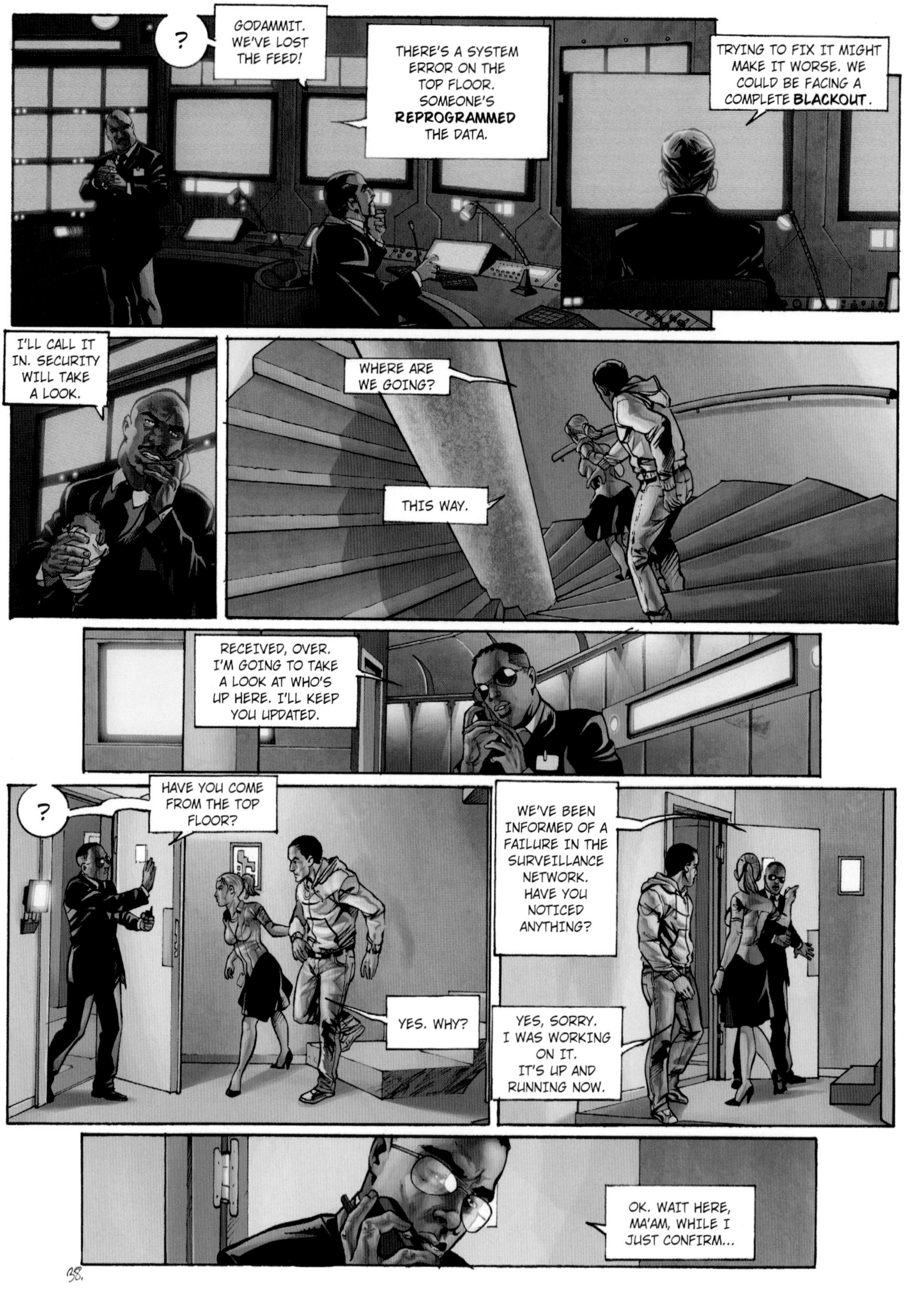
?
GODAMMIT. WE'VE LOST THE FEED!
THERE'S A SYSTEM ERROR ON THE TOP FLOOR. SOMEONE'S **REPROGRAMMED** THE DATA.
TRYING TO FIX IT MIGHT MAKE IT WORSE. WE COULD BE FACING A COMPLETE **BLACKOUT**.
I'LL CALL IT IN. SECURITY WILL TAKE A LOOK.
WHERE ARE WE GOING?
THIS WAY.
RECEIVED, OVER. I'M GOING TO TAKE A LOOK AT WHO'S UP HERE. I'LL KEEP YOU UPDATED.
?
HAVE YOU COME FROM THE TOP FLOOR?
YES. WHY?
WE'VE BEEN INFORMED OF A FAILURE IN THE SURVEILLANCE NETWORK. HAVE YOU NOTICED ANYTHING?
YES, SORRY. I WAS WORKING ON IT. IT'S UP AND RUNNING NOW.
OK. WAIT HERE, MA'AM, WHILE I JUST CONFIRM...
38.

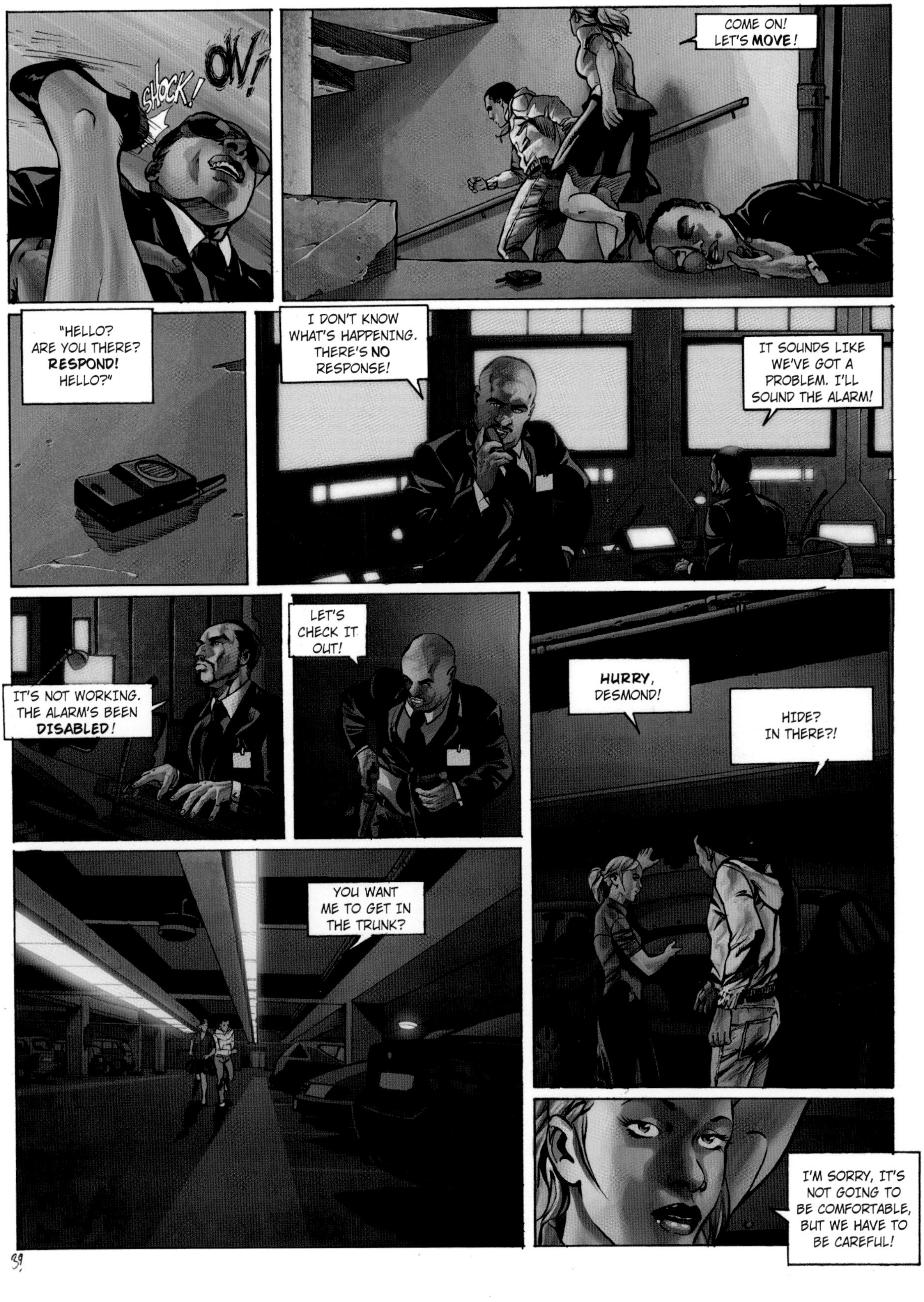
SHOCK!
ON!
COME ON! LET'S MOVE!
"HELLO? ARE YOU THERE? RESPOND! HELLO?"
I DON'T KNOW WHAT'S HAPPENING. THERE'S NO RESPONSE!
IT SOUNDS LIKE WE'VE GOT A PROBLEM. I'LL SOUND THE ALARM!
IT'S NOT WORKING. THE ALARM'S BEEN DISABLED!
LET'S CHECK IT OUT!
HURRY, DESMOND!
HIDE? IN THERE?!
YOU WANT ME TO GET IN THE TRUNK?
I'M SORRY, IT'S NOT GOING TO BE COMFORTABLE, BUT WE HAVE TO BE CAREFUL!
39

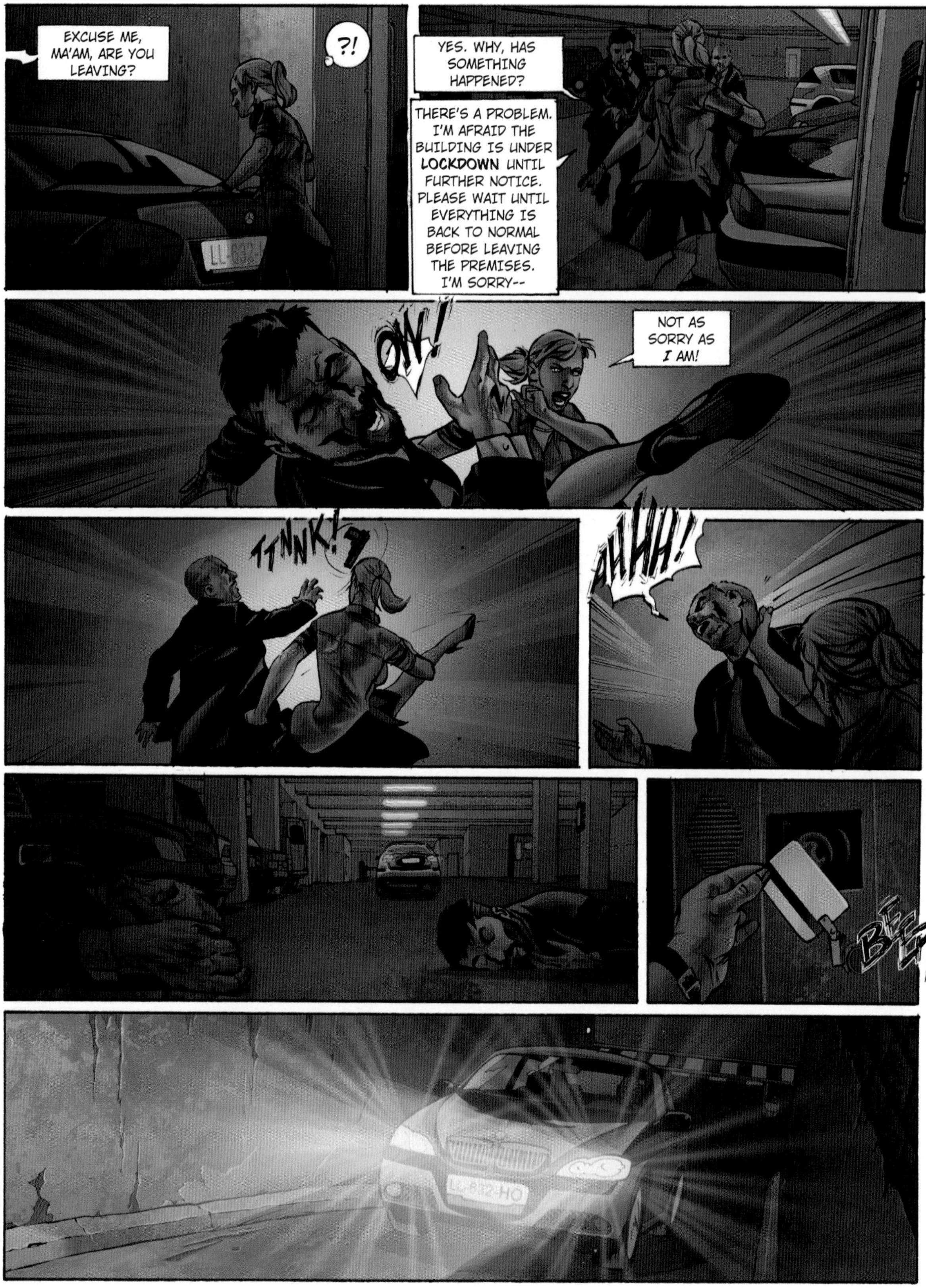
EXCUSE ME, MA'AM, ARE YOU LEAVING?
?!
YES. WHY, HAS SOMETHING HAPPENED?
THERE'S A PROBLEM. I'M AFRAID THE BUILDING IS UNDER LOCKDOWN UNTIL FURTHER NOTICE. PLEASE WAIT UNTIL EVERYTHING IS BACK TO NORMAL BEFORE LEAVING THE PREMISES. I'M SORRY--
OW!
NOT AS SORRY AS I AM!
TTNNK!
AHHH!
BEEP!
LL-632-HO

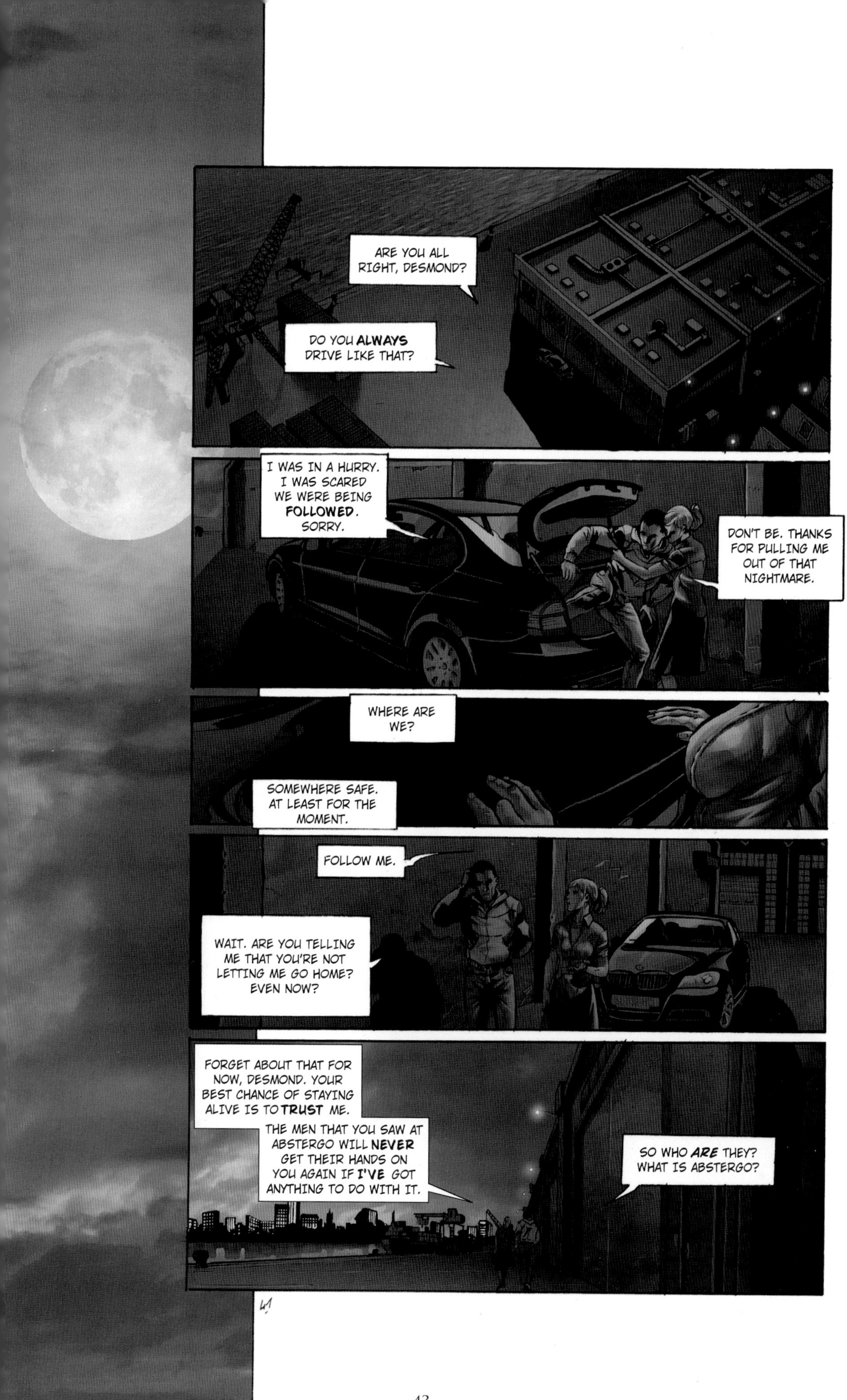
ARE YOU ALL RIGHT, DESMOND?
DO YOU **ALWAYS** DRIVE LIKE THAT?
I WAS IN A HURRY. I WAS SCARED WE WERE BEING **FOLLOWED**. SORRY.
DON'T BE. THANKS FOR PULLING ME OUT OF THAT NIGHTMARE.
WHERE ARE WE?
SOMEWHERE SAFE. AT LEAST FOR THE MOMENT.
FOLLOW ME.
WAIT. ARE YOU TELLING ME THAT YOU'RE NOT LETTING ME GO HOME? EVEN NOW?
FORGET ABOUT THAT FOR NOW, DESMOND. YOUR BEST CHANCE OF STAYING ALIVE IS TO **TRUST** ME.
THE MEN THAT YOU SAW AT ABSTERGO WILL **NEVER** GET THEIR HANDS ON YOU AGAIN IF **I'VE** GOT ANYTHING TO DO WITH IT.
SO WHO ***ARE*** THEY? WHAT IS ABSTERGO?
41

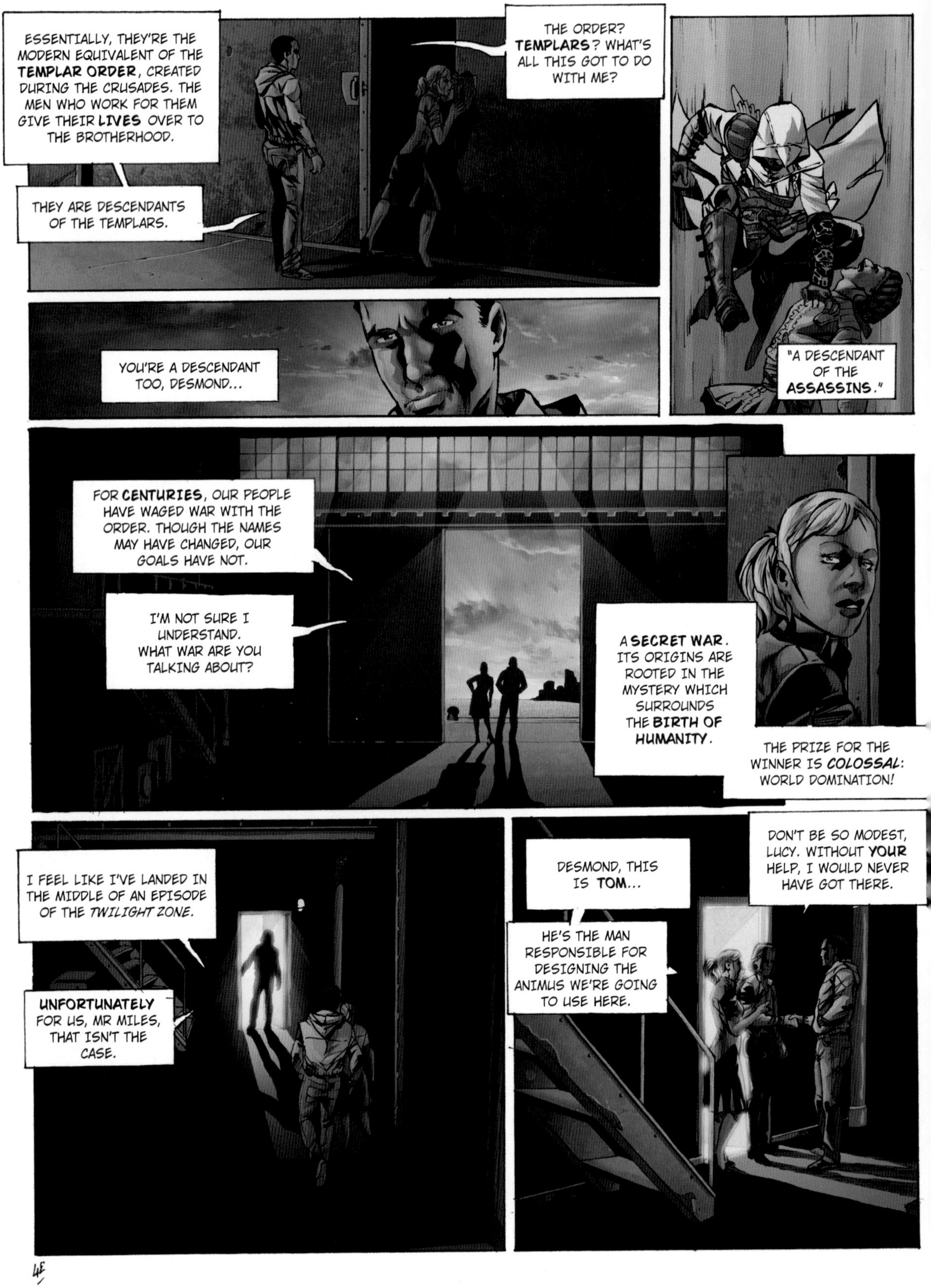
ESSENTIALLY, THEY'RE THE MODERN EQUIVALENT OF THE TEMPLAR ORDER, CREATED DURING THE CRUSADES. THE MEN WHO WORK FOR THEM GIVE THEIR LIVES OVER TO THE BROTHERHOOD.
THEY ARE DESCENDANTS OF THE TEMPLARS.
THE ORDER? TEMPLARS? WHAT'S ALL THIS GOT TO DO WITH ME?
YOU'RE A DESCENDANT TOO, DESMOND...
"A DESCENDANT OF THE ASSASSINS."
FOR CENTURIES, OUR PEOPLE HAVE WAGED WAR WITH THE ORDER. THOUGH THE NAMES MAY HAVE CHANGED, OUR GOALS HAVE NOT.
I'M NOT SURE I UNDERSTAND. WHAT WAR ARE YOU TALKING ABOUT?
A SECRET WAR. ITS ORIGINS ARE ROOTED IN THE MYSTERY WHICH SURROUNDS THE BIRTH OF HUMANITY.
THE PRIZE FOR THE WINNER IS COLOSSAL: WORLD DOMINATION!
I FEEL LIKE I'VE LANDED IN THE MIDDLE OF AN EPISODE OF THE TWILIGHT ZONE.
UNFORTUNATELY FOR US, MR MILES, THAT ISN'T THE CASE.
DESMOND, THIS IS TOM...
HE'S THE MAN RESPONSIBLE FOR DESIGNING THE ANIMUS WE'RE GOING TO USE HERE.
DON'T BE SO MODEST, LUCY. WITHOUT YOUR HELP, I WOULD NEVER HAVE GOT THERE.

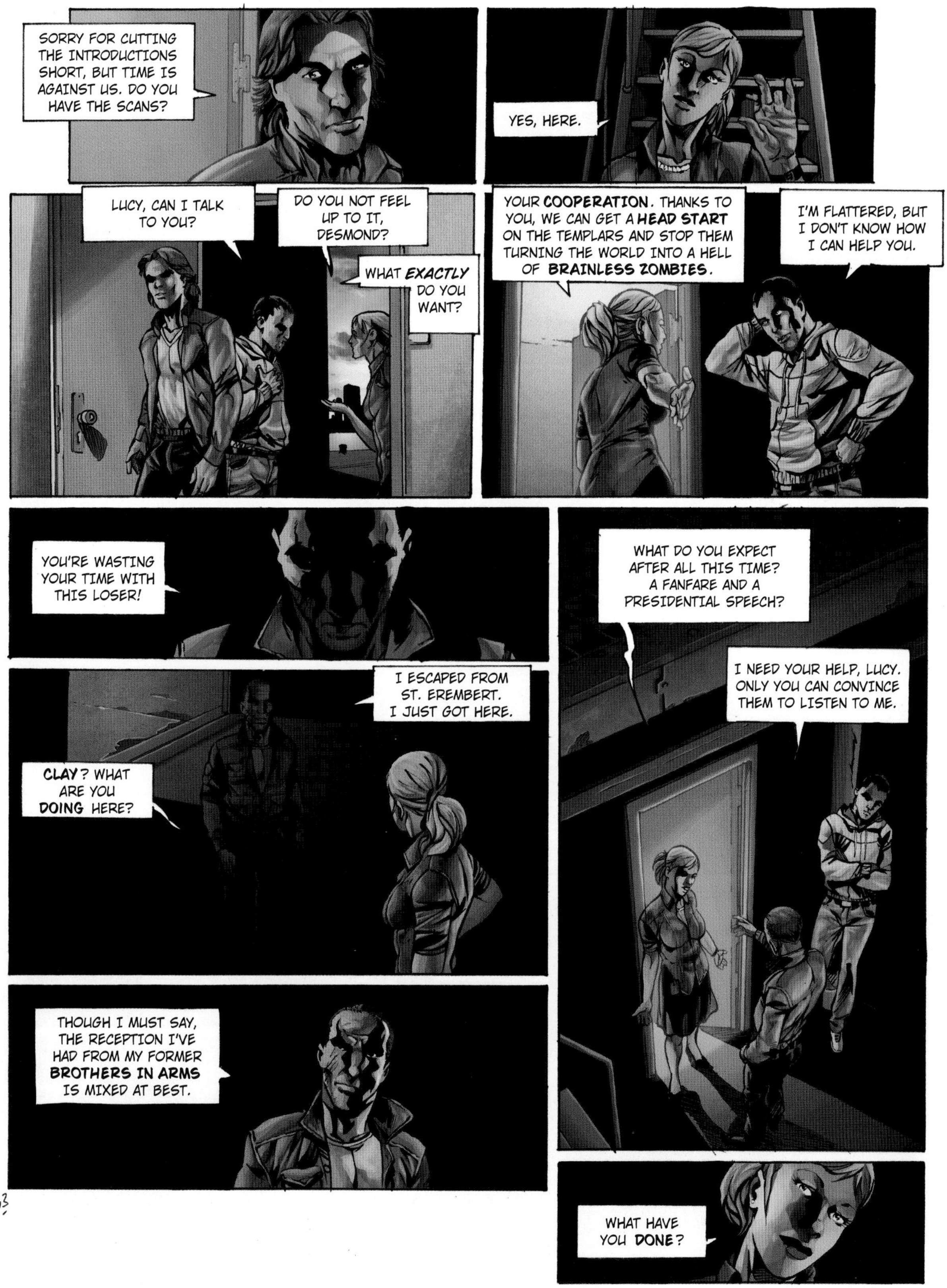
SORRY FOR CUTTING THE INTRODUCTIONS SHORT, BUT TIME IS AGAINST US. DO YOU HAVE THE SCANS?
YES, HERE.
LUCY, CAN I TALK TO YOU?
DO YOU NOT FEEL UP TO IT, DESMOND?
WHAT EXACTLY DO YOU WANT?
YOUR COOPERATION. THANKS TO YOU, WE CAN GET A HEAD START ON THE TEMPLARS AND STOP THEM TURNING THE WORLD INTO A HELL OF BRAINLESS ZOMBIES.
I'M FLATTERED, BUT I DON'T KNOW HOW I CAN HELP YOU.
YOU'RE WASTING YOUR TIME WITH THIS LOSER!
I ESCAPED FROM ST. EREMBERT. I JUST GOT HERE.
CLAY? WHAT ARE YOU DOING HERE?
THOUGH I MUST SAY, THE RECEPTION I'VE HAD FROM MY FORMER BROTHERS IN ARMS IS MIXED AT BEST.
WHAT DO YOU EXPECT AFTER ALL THIS TIME? A FANFARE AND A PRESIDENTIAL SPEECH?
I NEED YOUR HELP, LUCY. ONLY YOU CAN CONVINCE THEM TO LISTEN TO ME.
WHAT HAVE YOU DONE?

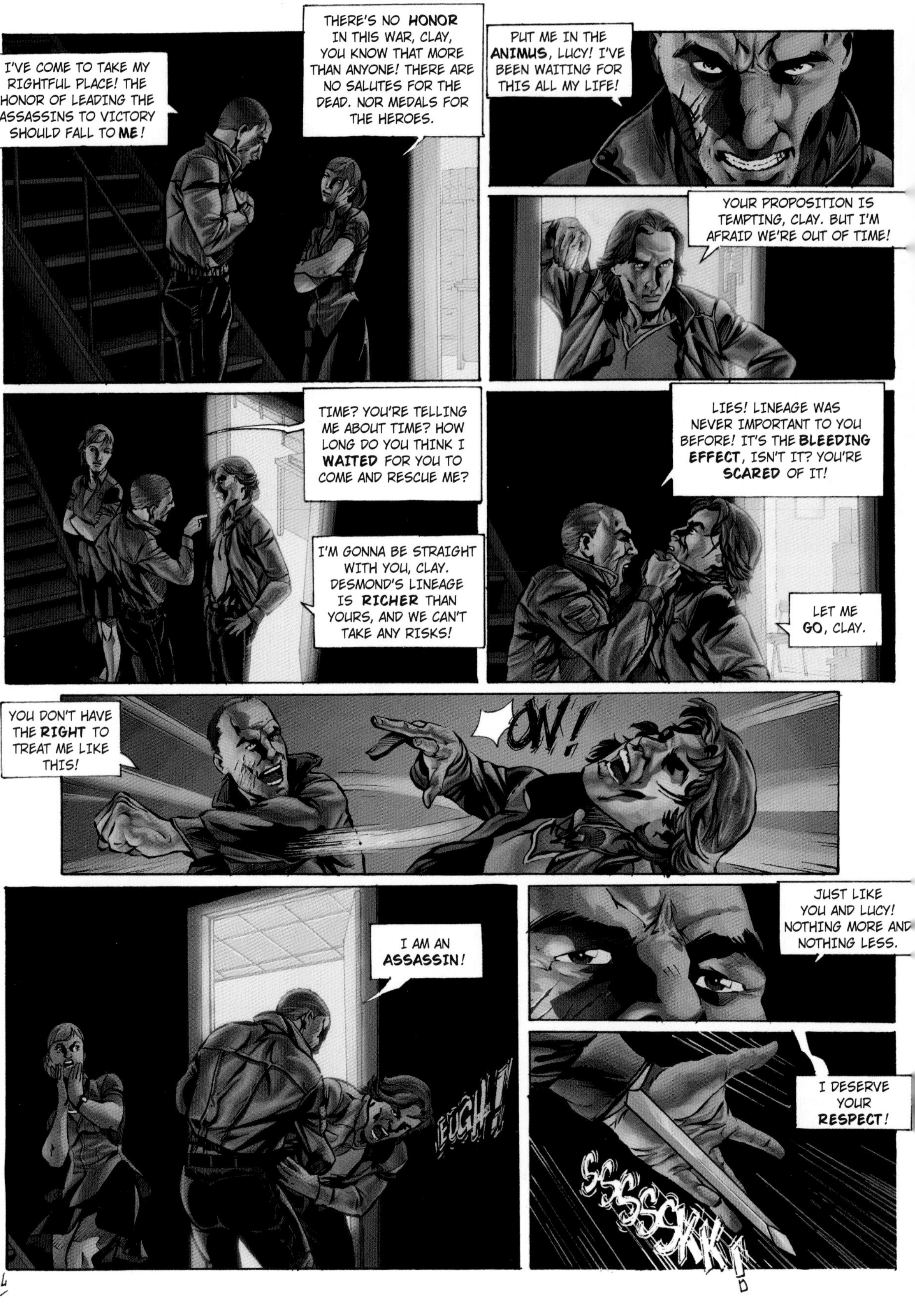
I'VE COME TO TAKE MY RIGHTFUL PLACE! THE HONOR OF LEADING THE ASSASSINS TO VICTORY SHOULD FALL TO **ME**!
THERE'S NO **HONOR** IN THIS WAR, CLAY, YOU KNOW THAT MORE THAN ANYONE! THERE ARE NO SALUTES FOR THE DEAD. NOR MEDALS FOR THE HEROES.
PUT ME IN THE **ANIMUS**, LUCY! I'VE BEEN WAITING FOR THIS ALL MY LIFE!
YOUR PROPOSITION IS TEMPTING, CLAY. BUT I'M AFRAID WE'RE OUT OF TIME!
TIME? YOU'RE TELLING ME ABOUT TIME? HOW LONG DO YOU THINK I **WAITED** FOR YOU TO COME AND RESCUE ME?
I'M GONNA BE STRAIGHT WITH YOU, CLAY. DESMOND'S LINEAGE IS **RICHER** THAN YOURS, AND WE CAN'T TAKE ANY RISKS!
LIES! LINEAGE WAS NEVER IMPORTANT TO YOU BEFORE! IT'S THE **BLEEDING EFFECT**, ISN'T IT? YOU'RE **SCARED** OF IT!
LET ME **GO**, CLAY.
YOU DON'T HAVE THE **RIGHT** TO TREAT ME LIKE THIS!
I AM AN **ASSASSIN**!
EUGH!
JUST LIKE YOU AND LUCY! NOTHING MORE AND NOTHING LESS.
I DESERVE YOUR **RESPECT**!

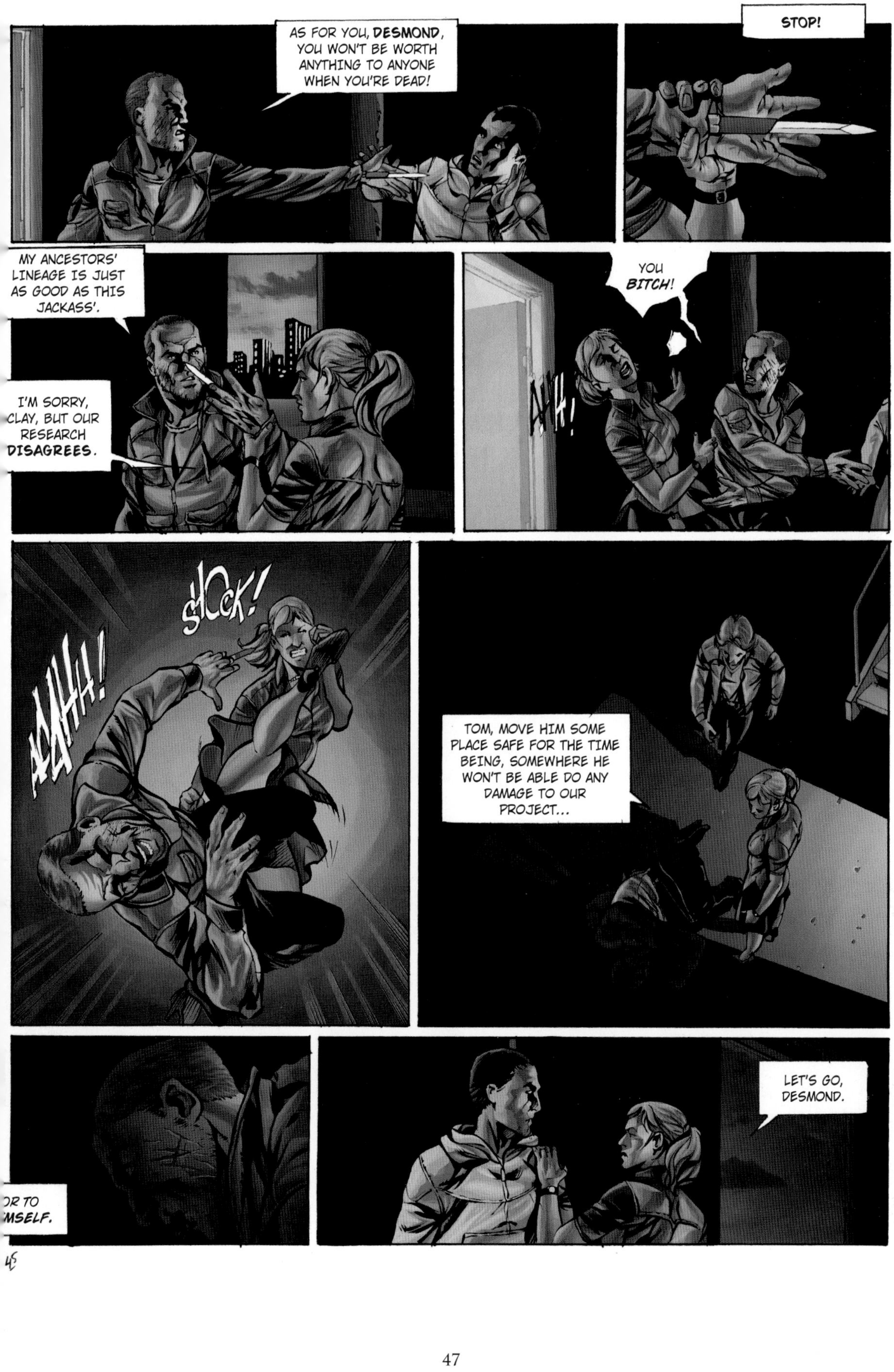
AS FOR YOU, DESMOND, YOU WON'T BE WORTH ANYTHING TO ANYONE WHEN YOU'RE DEAD!
STOP!
MY ANCESTORS' LINEAGE IS JUST AS GOOD AS THIS JACKASS'.
I'M SORRY, CLAY, BUT OUR RESEARCH DISAGREES.
YOU BITCH!
AAHH!
SHOCK!
AAAHH!
TOM, MOVE HIM SOME PLACE SAFE FOR THE TIME BEING, SOMEWHERE HE WON'T BE ABLE DO ANY DAMAGE TO OUR PROJECT...
LET'S GO, DESMOND.

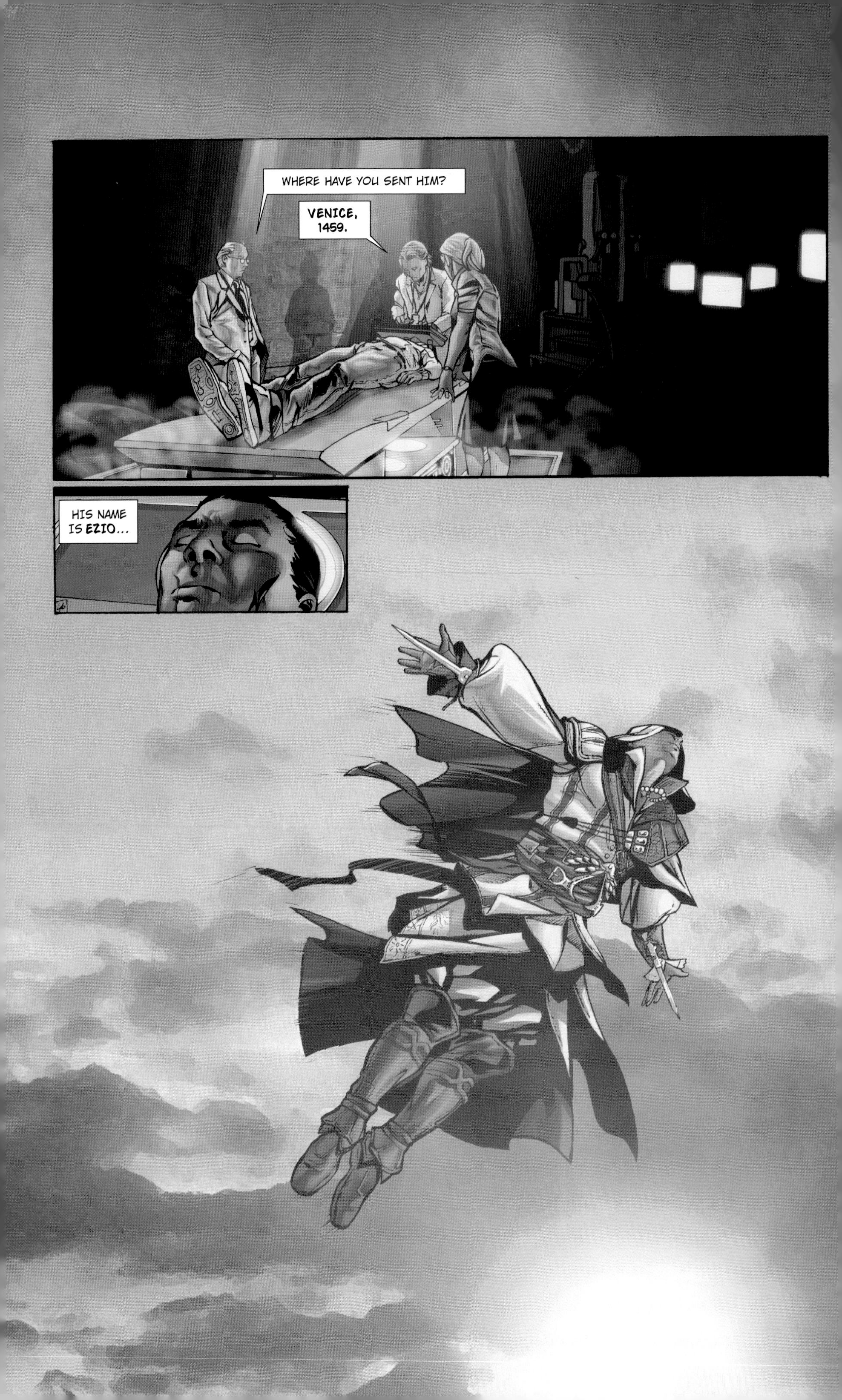
WHERE HAVE YOU SENT HIM?
VENICE, 1459.
HIS NAME IS EZIO...